Parish Catechumenate:
Pastors, Presiders, Preachers

Font and Table Series

The *Font and Table Series* offers pastoral perspectives on Christian baptism, confirmation and eucharist. Other titles in the series are:

A Catechumenate Needs Everybody: Study Guides for Parish Ministers

An Easter Sourcebook: The Fifty Days

Baptism Is a Beginning

Before and After Baptism: The Work of Teachers and Catechists

Commentaries on the Rite of Christian Initiation of Adults

Confirmation: A Parish Celebration

Finding and Forming Sponsors and Godparents

Guide for Sponsors

How Does a Person Become a Catholic?

How to Form a Catechumenate Team

Infant Baptism in the Parish: Understanding the Rite

Welcoming the New Catholic

Related and available through Liturgy Training Publications:

The Rite of Christian Initiation of Adults (Ritual Edition)

The Rite of Christian Initiation of Adults (Study Edition)

Parish Catechumenate:

Pastors, Presiders, Preachers

Edited by James A. Wilde

Liturgy Training Publications

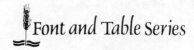

Font and Table Series

GENERAL EDITOR
James A. Wilde

EDITORIAL CONSULTANTS
Allan Bouley, OSB, professor of liturgy
St. John's University
Collegeville MN

Frank T. Griswold, bishop
Episcopal Diocese of Chicago
Chicago IL

Elizabeth Jeep, author and consultant
River Forest IL

Gordon Lathrop, professor of liturgy
Lutheran Theological Seminary
Philadelphia PA

Ron Lewinski, director
Office for Divine Worship
Catholic Archdiocese of Chicago
Chicago IL

ACKNOWLEDGMENTS

Excerpts from *Rite of Christian Initiation of Adults,* copyright © 1985,
International Committee on English in the Liturgy, Inc.
Washington DC. All rights reserved.

Excerpts from *Poems* by Jessica Powers, OCD, copyright © 1987,
Carmel of the Mother of God, Pewaukee WI. Used with permission.
All rights reserved.

Liturgy Training Publications
1800 North Hermitage Avenue
Chicago IL 60622-1101

Order Phone: 312/486-7008
Editorial Phone: 312/486-8970

Printed in the United States

ISBN 0-930467-85-X

Cover and book design: Jane Kremsreiter
Cover painting: Linda Ekstrom

Contents

Foreword

AS OUR UNDERSTANDING and experience of the parish catechumenate continues to grow, the areas that require more attention are the roles of pastors, preachers and presiders. Pastors exercise considerable influence on a catechumenate because, as leaders charged with overseeing the complete spiritual care of a parish, pastors can integrate the catechumenate into the fabric of life of the whole community. Some pastors see parishioners taking more responsibility for the initiation of new members and sadly conclude that they no longer are needed for the process. Unfortunate! Pastors can exercise significant spiritual leadership in assuring that the vision of the catechumenate permeates all parish life. We need pastors to empower and support the full network of catechumenate ministries.

Although the role of the diocesan bishop could be the subject for another book in this series, one needs to acknowledge that the bishop's pastoral leadership and personal involvement in the initiation of adults will, in turn, affect the pastors of the diocese. As chief pastor of the local church, the bishop could easily apply the contents of this publication to his episcopal ministry, as the article "What

Kind of Spiritual Leaders Does the Catechumenate Want?" by Robert F. Morneau, auxiliary bishop of Green Bay, will show.

The articles by Thomas J. Caroluzza offer an overview of a pastor's role and collaborative ministry and answer the important question regarding the size of a community from a pastor's perspective. Because a pastor does not exercise office in isolation, Mary Benet McKinney's description of practical ways to share ministries will be valuable to study.

All the articles in *Parish Catechumenate: Pastors, Presiders, Preachers* should spark pastors' reflections on their own ministry in light of the catechumenate. This book will not answer all questions or give a once-and-for-all definition of the pastor's role. But it begins a dialogue, desperately needed if the catechumenate is going to continue to mature in a healthy manner.

I have met many ordained pastors who feel somewhat unsure about their role and their value in the catechumenate process. Much like the documents of Vatican II, which said very little about the pastor, the RCIA is not very explicit about the pastor's unique contribution. This, in turn, may explain why some clergy were ambivalent toward or sluggish in accepting the catechumenate even when their parishioners who attended an institute or workshop came home eager to work with their pastor. From the broad strokes of the ritual book through articles such as these and through ongoing reflection, the role of the pastor continues to be refined.

Presiders and preachers also need to look a second time at how vital their roles are in the formation and initiation of new members. When one considers that the word of God is the school of Christian formation for the catechumen, the preacher cannot help but view preaching as an essential component. Remember, too, that preaching does take place only at Sunday liturgy. "What Kind of Lenten Homilies Does the Catechumenate Want?" by Austin H. Fleming and "What Kind of Eastertime Homilies Does the Catechumenate Want?" by James T. Telthorst both make sensitive, pointed and profound observations about what happens during an average homily and what can happen during a good homily.

Presiding should not be regarded as a mere function someone must perform to get through the rites. The style and grace of the presider may say as much to catechumens and the assembly about what we're doing in the rites as the words of the rites themselves. Robert Hovda provides the presider ample food for clear thought in "What Kind of Presider Does the Catechumenate Want?" He knows that effective liturgical presiding follows correct liturgical understanding, coupled with a solid liturgical spirituality.

When both preaching and presiding, interest in and love for the catechumens will make a world of difference in how effective these special ministries become.

As special as the ministry of pastor, presider or preacher is, I would hope that these ministries do not become so specialized that their interconnectedness and their link to the whole is lost. At the same time, I hope that this book brings encouragement and affirmation to those who already have been struggling to exercise the ministry of pastoring, presiding and preaching. With the experience of the catechumenate in one hand and the contents of this book in the other, pastors, presiders and preachers should find much about which to be hopeful.

◆ *Ron Lewinski*

Preface

OW CAN ANYONE say that the catechumenate wants something? That someone wants to be a catechumen, that a catechumen wants something or that a parish wants a catechumenate is easily understandable, but how can a catechumenate "want" anything?

In 1976 the late Ralph A. Keifer placed the question in its broadest perspective:

> The attempt to reform the rites of initiation has issued in the promulgation of rites which are, historically and culturally speaking, a massive rejection of the presuppositions both of pastoral practice and of most churchgoers regarding the true meaning of church membership. This is a revolution quite without precedent because the Catholic church has never at any time in its history done such violence to its ritual practice as to make its rites so wholly incongruous with its concrete reality. Such an act is either a statement that rite is wholly irrelevant, or a statement that the church is willing to change, and to change radically, that concrete reality. Such an approach is either suicide or prophecy of a very high order.[1]

If the prophecy of an ecumenical council with the approval of the Holy See and the signature of the Roman pontiff is to be fulfilled, the restored catechumenate cries out for the church to change radically. Pastors, presiders and preachers are among the first to hear the cry.

If we open ourselves to the church's need for a renewed spiritual leadership, a genuinely collaborative ministry, a liturgical presiding manner that is "strong, loving and wise," a homiletic style that reflects personal faith and a willingness to wrestle with the word in all its power to enlighten our weak world—if we open our ears to that, we are choosing life for the church.

If we open our hearts to people seeking God's love through Christ in their still-to-come or their once-upon-a-time baptism, we become prophets for the church. If the mystery of Lent, Triduum and Eastertime is central to our prayer in private and in public, and if that mystery is central to parish prayer in the same way, then the church will rise to the challenge of the prophets. If our preaching by word and example is faithful to the signs and times, and if it is central to our life and the ministry of the parish, God's good news will be heard in the assembly.

That is how the catechumenate can want something. That is what the catechumenate wants.

♦ *James A. Wilde, editor*

Notes

1. Ralph A. Keifer, "Christian Initiation: The State of the Question," in *Made, Not Born: New Perspectives on Christian Initiation and the Catechumenate,* from the Murphy Center for Liturgical Research (Notre Dame, Indiana: University of Notre Dame Press, 1976), 149-50.

What Kind of Pastor Does the Catechumenate Want?

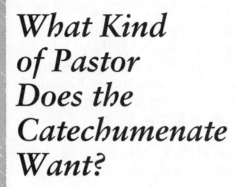

T HAPPENED TO ME this year on the fourth of our church's seven Easter Sundays. I was seated in the presider's chair, listening to a woman who had taken over the pulpit! This was not a reactionary seige nor some angry response to grace. It was the public witness of someone who survived the plunge into the baptismal waters at the Easter Vigil. She was a neophyte who was compelled to give testimony before us old-time Catholics about her newfound faith. Neither I nor most Catholics in white, suburban America are accustomed to this kind of witness.

As I listened to the true story of how a life had changed, as I heard the excitement in her voice, as I listened to the conviction and joy of this formerly shy, timid woman, as I heard her talk about the need to serve in our church—as I heard that, I was deeply moved. If I were to label my feelings, I'd say they were basically feelings of gratitude for what God was up to in this old church of ours.

This is one of many examples over the years that has led me to realize that the Rite of Christian Initiation of Adults (RCIA) was succeeding in reshaping the church and re-forming its members where many other efforts have met with only limited success. After 13 years of experience with the catechumenate in three different parishes, I know that it is doing more to help us understand the church and be the church than the many books, lectures, tapes, programs and homilies about the church that have come out since Vatican Council II. The rich images, models and analogues from theologians have been helpful in moving certain people to a fuller appreciation of the mystery that we call church, but those images have not yet succeeded in reaching most of the people in our pews. What is teaching us about the church is the well-practiced rite of Christian initiation. It is gradually and carefully reshaping the American parish. As more and more parishioners celebrate and experience a journey of faith with catechumens, they gradually come to a fuller awareness of the church.

We might have predicted that it would happen this way. Lasting insights, insights that make a difference in how we live in our day-to-day world of family, friends, work and leisure, come to us through ritual: the connection between church and home—the actions, words and symbols that bridge them together.

What I want to share with you are some specific ways in which I believe our church is being reshaped by the catechumenate. There are many more, but here are a few.

The Pastoral Smell for a Good Thing

As I look back over these past 13 years, I am struck by the great number of parish priests and ministers who realized instinctively the power of this rite to re-form us. Even with a limited experience with the rite, they began to see its implications for everything that they did in the parish ministry. The parishes that experienced a good catechumenate began to add a catechumenal "flavor" to everything else that they did. When they witnessed its power in the lives of catechumens, they began to translate and accommodate the rite for other purposes. "Why not include in the catechumenate sessions those parishioners who want to update themselves?" "How about a catechumenate for teens and those preparing for confirmation?" "Wouldn't this same process work for parents preparing their children for baptism, first eucharist and first penance?" Finally, some, including myself, began to ask: "Why not invite every Catholic in the parish into a quasi-catechumenate? Isn't this the best way to conduct contemporary adult education?"

Responding to these hunches, many pastors and other parish ministers in the early 1980s began to see a potential inquirer hiding behind every missalette. While the intuition that prompted this inflated catechumenate may have been correct, and while action on such intuitions produced marvelous results, some negative, unforeseen side effects also arose: The blurring of distinctions between the baptized but uncatechized on the one hand and the catechumens on the other tended to dilute the power of the rite. At times the words, gestures and symbols became inappropriate and unauthentic. Worse still, the "all-inclusive catechumenate" really was distracting us from evangelizing the hundreds and sometimes thousands of unchurched people in our neighborhoods.

The pastoral smell for a good thing was basically correct. It took thoughtful experience and good ministry to convince most of us that the principles underlying the rite could influence and refashion our parish work without wholesale borrowing or blatant mimicry.

The Catechumenate Continually Challenges a Parish

The catechumenate, we found, would work its power on us more effectively in subtle and indirect ways. What we learned was that its primary power to reshape the parish was in the ongoing challenge that the catechumens and neophytes presented to "veteran" parishioners. It was the week-by-week contact with inquirers, catechumens, elect and neophytes that re-formed us. As we watched them grow in zeal, we began to take stock of our own brand of discipleship. As we heard the stories of new discoveries, some of our old matter-of-factness about faith was challenged. As fresh faith was displayed, stale faith stood out for what it was. As we came face-to-face with new energy, dedication, childlike awe and wonder, old routines were confronted, unholy habits were uncovered, burned-out fervor was enkindled, cynicism and loss of aspiration was exposed. Most of all, trivial parish preoccupations were called into question.

This power of the catechumenate is no quick fix, to be sure. Its power is for the long haul. Its way of reshaping the church will endure and stand the test of time. The catechumenate fosters the gradual unfolding of the mystery of the church lived today, handed on for tomorrow.

A Catechumenate Mirrors the Parish

When the adult catechumenate becomes the way of life in a parish, when the catechumens are not the concern of just a few privileged pastoral staff members, when all parishioners make the catechumenate their business as the RCIA suggests, then the catechumenate will wield its power over us. It will mirror who we are as a church and who we are called to become. It will shout out to us singly and corporately that we are called to ongoing conversion. We no longer can be content to remain the same people, patterning the same old ways year after year.

An obvious place to begin is with the sacrament of baptism. The catechumenate has helped parishioners rethink the meaning of their baptisms and the baptisms of their children. As they hear the neophytes speak of their own baptisms as radical experiences that make them single-minded, determined and ready to spend their lives in witness and service, then cultural christenings make little sense. The neophyte challenges old definitions and former practices of baptism: no more vague spiritual vaccination against future unnamed demons. Trickling a few drops of water over the forehead may have sufficed for validity in the past, but that practice soon comes into question when catechumens begin to model for us the radical sign of dying and rising in the water.

We have a history of trivializing our baptism, making it into a passive membership. We lost the sense of baptism's radical call to discipleship. The renewal of our baptismal profession at Easter can take on new meaning for us old Catholics when done so close to the plunge of the catechumens into the waters of the font that night. We begin to understand what Tertullian meant when he spoke of infant baptism, our baptism, not as an event but as a "direction for our lives," an orientation. In the Vigil we become aware of our need to renew its meaning for our lives.

What's happening to baptism for parishioners in catechumenal parishes is something like that which happened to the young boy who was brought to the monastery during medieval times. He was given a robe that was much too large for him; he was swallowed up in it. So they gave him a cord to pull it up and tuck it in. The child was expected to grow into the robe, to let it out and down as he grew. The robe wasn't expected to fit right away. The catechumenate shows us that the name Christian and the mission of a disciple is something that we grow into. It is true that we, like the boy novice, receive the whole thing at our baptism, all the incipient gifts of the Spirit, but that call and mission unfold in us year by year. The catechumenate helps us to understand our baptism in a new way: to take delight day by day in our ongoing conversion, the ever-fuller expression and practice of our once-upon-a-time baptism.

Collaborative Ministry

The catechumenate models for us the implications of baptism for ministry. An excellent practical articulation of Vatican II's call for a renewal of ministry can be found in the Rite itself. The collaborative ministry outlined in the RCIA is the core of the catechumenate. Furthermore, according to the 1983 Code of Canon Law, pastoral councils are optional in parishes, *but according to liturgical law, the adult catechumenate is not.* We may conclude, therefore, that a ministerially collaborative church that is reflected powerfully in the catechumenate is mandated for all parishes.

What are some of the features of ministerial collaboration? We read in the RCIA that collaborative ministry has a ripple effect in a parish. What began to strike me early on was the frequent actual or implied use of the preposition *with* when the role of the pastor was described. A few examples will illustrate the point:

— "During the period [of inquiry], priests and deacons, catechists and other laypersons, are to give the candidates a suitable explanation of the gospel." (RCIA, 38)

— "An inquirer or 'sympathizer' is introduced by a friend and then welcomed and received by the priest or some other representative member of the community." (RCIA, 39)

— "There must be evidence of the first stirrings of repentance, a start to the practice of calling upon God in prayer, a sense of the church and some experience of the company and spirit of Christians through contact with a priest or with members of the community." (RCIA, 42)

— "With the help of the sponsors, catechists and deacons, parish priests (pastors) have the responsibility for judging the outward indications of [the inquirers'] dispositions." (RCIA, 43)

— "A suitable catechesis is provided by priests or deacons, or by catechists and others of the faithful." (RCIA, 75)

Obviously, the text envisions the priest as someone who exercises his ministry collaboratively with a variety of other ministers. The RCIA articulates a practical theology of ministry for the church. Further, catechumenal practice shows that the church is first of all a *local* church with people gathered in parish and home. This practice also demonstrates that there is no church, even locally, without the bishop.

Ripples in the Larger Church

The bishop is the one who calls the elect on the First Sunday of Lent. The bishop meets with neophytes on his parish visitation. To some, these may appear to be minimal deferences to his authority, but in practice they have proved to be a major corrective to congregationalism. No one feels the impact of these seemingly insignificant practices more than the catechumens themselves. These are teachable moments for them: "I wanted to join Holy Spirit parish, but who is this man?" Once again, we do not begin with doctrine but with experiences and questions such as these. "Who is he for you?" we might ask. "As you saw and spoke with catechumens from every part of the diocese at the Rite of Election, did you have a sense that you belong to something much bigger than Holy Spirit parish?" Invariably the answer is "yes." Now we can tell them about the office of bishop in our church. Now they can learn in convincing and lasting ways the meaning of collegiality, catholicity, magisterium, even infallibility. They first *experienced* the bishop as teacher, overseer, link to the universal church; now we can teach them.

The adult catechumenate helps us to define not only the role of bishop and pastor but also the role of lay people whom it calls into collaborative ministry. They are charged with living out their baptism more fully by practicing a biblical hospitality with every stranger. They are called to be listeners to people's stories, inquiring and raising questions in order to connect those stories with the great story of the church. This is to be done not so much out of a book but out of the real experience of life.

As lay people or clergy uncover the first promptings of grace in the lives of inquirers and catechumens, they see more of what it means to be a follower of Jesus and member of the church. In short, they learn about ministry by ministering in the catechumenate. Sponsors and catechists experience this in a heightened way. That is why it is our practice to include as many parishioners as possible in these roles. Every year more parishioners are given this opportunity to grow through service in the catechumenate. A vision of the church shaped by the catechumenate demands that we never allow initiation to become the specialty of a few of us, but rather the ministry of all.

With four annual retreats for catechumens, each involving different parishioners; with still other parishioners organizing social events; with others caring for inquirers in an ongoing precatechumenate; with a pool of sponsors and a team of catechists ministering to the needs of candidates—with all of this happening, the catechumenate soon becomes the business of all the faithful. "The entire community must help the candidates and the catechumens throughout the process of initiation: during the period of the precatechumenate, the period of the catechumenate, the period of purification and enlightenment and the period of postbaptismal catechesis or mystagogy." (RCIA, 9) But there are hundreds of others who still will lack this beneficial, close relationship with the inquirers, catechumens and neophytes. We can gain some of this involvement through the careful and reverent celebration of the rites, helping all parishioners to understand their role in them. All must be challenged to create a climate that nurtures this new faith. All must be a part of the scrutinies and exorcisms, realizing that these first reorientations toward the reign of God and away from the reign of Satan challenge us to an ongoing commitment. We longtime Catholics still play around with anti-reign-of-God ideas such as racism, sexism, militarism, privatism and consumerism. We become captivated by this other way of life and therefore must get on our knees with the elect every Lent and allow ourselves to be scrutinized and exorcised from these subtle captivations. These and the other rites will draw all of us into a closer relationship with the catechumens.

Our parish goes a step further in this effort of inclusion. Catechumens and neophytes become members of different small communities where many parishioners have the opportunity to experience and participate in their special time of grace.

These are a few ways that the parish is being reshaped by the catechumenate. Gradually, the catechumenate is teaching us what it means to be a church, by deepening our understanding of baptism and by renewing our commitment to ministry. We're learning that the church can come alive in our time through the new members the Lord sends into our midst. But isn't that the way it's meant to be? Aren't families radically altered every time there's the birth of another child? Doesn't the new child challenge the parents and siblings to new ways of relating, new ways of being, new ways of loving and serving? Doesn't all the attention demanded by this new life in the family tap into our dormant reserves of life, energy and generous love, and doesn't this new child reshape our human families? The family and its spirit lives on in its progeny; it does not die.

In reality, when a new life is added to a family, the family itself becomes a new person. Synergy rather than mathematics takes over. The whole becomes *more* than the sum of the parts. Members draw deeply on previously unknown personal resources within them when a child is born. Each individual becomes richer, and so does the whole. Changes occur not only within the family but between the family and the rest of the world. Certainly the birth of an exceptional child brings out this new family personality most dramatically, but the birth of any child makes the family a new, richer person, and through it, the whole human family becomes a new person.

The family of the church similarly is challenged to become pregnant with new life, to provide excellent prenatal care, to take pains to prepare the older siblings for the challenging but happy change that is soon to take place among us and to rejoice that we are being refashioned by new life into a fuller sign of the reign of God. This is a sufficient reason for any of us to take over the pulpits of our churches and proclaim loudly and clearly from these pulpits where we work and live and play that God's up to something marvelous in our time: We are alive with Easter faith. Come and see. Watch God remake us into a credible sign of God's reign.

♦ *Thomas J. Caroluzza*

What Kind of Presider Does the Catechumenate Want?

OUR ANSWER to that title question is also a description of the kind of bishop and presbyter that the church wants and needs at any time and in any place. For bishops and presbyters are pastors and necessary presiders in the climax of the pastoral role: the Sunday eucharistic assembly. Deacons and other baptized Christians may and should preside in some of our other liturgical rites, but the one who has been engaged in the pastoral building up of the faith community, in encouraging and eliciting and enabling the different gifts of its different members, is the one who presides in their central sacrificial sacrament.

This makes good ecclesial sense, for the specialized ministries of bishop and presbyter are both collegial offices, relating the local church to the other churches. Every bishop is a member of the college of bishops, with the bishop of Rome presiding, and every presbyter is a member of a college of presbyters, with a bishop presiding. No bishop or presbyter functions properly apart from this relatedness (another reason for the urgency of the ecumenical movement). So the collegial character of their pastoral roles makes them important personal signs both of the oneness of their own church and of the communion among the churches. One of the Roman Catholic gifts to the ecumenical enterprise is the fact that Catholic unity is so jealous in its care for these personal signs and colleges, as well as for the more generally appreciated agents of Christian unity, such as the Bible, the sacraments and other rites, the historic creeds, the moral quest for justice and peace.

Before any specialized ministry within the church, however, is the church itself and the basic, general ministry of the entire body of Christ. The whole church is primary minister in both worship and mission. Ecclesiology has priority and the conciliar reform of revolution in our self-understanding as church naturally precedes reforms in the specialized ministries that serve the church's needs. Since the Second Vatican Council we have been trying, with more or less diligence, to absorb, implement and develop its teaching on the church. Today it looks like it may be a while before we get to the reforms for which our clergy situation pleads, to a gospel critique of customs relating to clergy qualifications, recruitment, nomination, election, training and life-style. The length and depth of our problems in this area are indicated by Cyrille Vogel in a Concilium volume that discusses the legitimizing of "absolute ordination" (ordination without a precise pastoral mission) several centuries ago: "This change at the end of the 12th century had as its major consequence a complete uprooting and dissociation of the clergy from the church."[1] It would be nice if all facets of ecclesial renewal could be polished and made to sparkle together again, but we are a slow and ornery lot.

The Rite of Christian Initiation of Adults (RCIA) is the most radical, most difficult and most necessary of all reforms that bear on the liturgy. The text of the RCIA assumes and teaches—and thereby revives—a very old ecclesiology that is new to most 20th-century Catholics, one in which the local church, the flesh-and-blood Sunday assembly, regains its place in our attention and concern. After centuries of obsession with the church's universal juridical and organizational aspects, the RCIA involves a new understanding of membership. Members who had been satisfied to consider themselves as consumers at any one of the local outlets of an international entity suddenly were invested with a dignity and responsibility quite foreign to the passive consumerism that had grown so comfortable for them.

So it is not at all surprising that even these beginnings of conciliar reform have been difficult for many and have aroused passionate reaction all the way from the church's leadership to its interested bystanders. The process of regaining a firmer footing on the pilgrim path may be halted for a moment, but it will not be reversed. Too much of our living tradition, with its roots and sources, has been glimpsed—if not yet recovered—to permit the survival of a top-heavy or pyramid ecclesiology.

That is why our answer to the question "What kind of presider does the catechumenate want?" must be a description of the kind of bishop and presbyter that the church needs everywhere and always. Such a description could be attempted in many different ways. For our purposes, I will follow the two relevant introductory documents of the liturgical book: the "General Introduction" of the Roman Ritual to "Christian Initiation" and the "Introduction" to the revised Rite of Christian Initiation of Adults.[2] Comments follow the relevant article numbers of those documents and quotations without footnotes are from the article indicated.

Christian Initiation: General Introduction

Presiders must see themselves, first of all, as *members* of the church, *members* of the Sunday assembly, with their primary dignity conferred in the sacraments of initiation. One cannot serve appropriately in any specialized ministry unless one is consciously and in a heartfelt manner a part of the community, aware of the radical egalitarianism implied by the gifts of initiation mentioned here: light, identification with Christ, filial relation to God and the right to "celebrate the memorial of the Lord's death and resurrection."

"Clergy" and "Laity." So the presider must escape the clericalism with which we still are burdened. Like America's racism, clericalism tends to survive in subtle ways even when we think we have outgrown it. When we speak of the Sunday assembly, then, we are speaking of the entire gathering of the baptized and presently

committed—specialized ministers and leaders, as well as all the rest. This fundamental truth has to be translated into appropriate feelings and attitudes on the part of the presider and all other leaders if it is to become the attitude of all. To regard the presider as an outsider, or as originating in a foreign clime or as separate from the assembly in any way, is to destroy the role.

A commentary on our currently revised ordination liturgy puts it clearly:

> To grasp the significance of this [revised rite] with regard to the source and origin of orders in the church and to the role of the ordained within the assembly, it must be stressed that nowhere in the revised rite of ordination is there a hint of a direct intervention by Christ that bypasses the action of the church assembled for prayer. Neither visually, symbolically nor verbally is there any intrusion on the action that appears to originate apart from the assembled church. If we are to maintain, as we must, that this act of ordination is an act of Christ, it becomes necessary to image it as an act of the Christ who is present in and as the assembled church and who acts when and as the church itself acts.[3]

Articles 2–6 of the General Introduction to Christian Initiation emphasize the transformation of candidates involved in the celebration of the sacraments of initiation, so that all the initiated are enabled to offer "themselves with Christ" and to be "offered to God by Christ their high priest" (2). Further, *all* are called and equipped "to carry out the mission of the entire people of God in the church and in the world" (2).

These rights, duties, dignities, mandates stem from initiation, not from ordination, and they apply to all initiates, including the clergy. There is no implication at all that church affairs are the province of the clergy and the world's secular affairs the province of the rest of the church. Quite the opposite. Because we are one, with the same basic union in Christ, both worship and mission are common to all of us. The presider who is not aware of this may feel an obligation—or worse, imagine a right—to be absent from the church's struggle for peace and justice in the world and to create a clerical ghetto. Christians who are not clergy (contemporary usage suggests getting rid of the term *laity* in all of its forms) likewise may experience a kind of hands-off imperative with regard to the worship and teaching and administrative life of the church. Such feelings and imaginings undermine our common mission.

The Presider's Socioeconomic Responsibilities. This does not mean that presiders can or should claim competence in specialized areas requiring technical knowledge and skill that they do not possess. It does mean that presiders are first of all human beings and members of the church and therefore share the church's work as well as worship. If presiders do not take seriously their political and economic and other social responsibilities, their specialized ministry will be weak and irrelevant. If presiders do not welcome and encourage the faith communities with which they work to a responsible and full participation in all church affairs, they are failing in their duty.

The appropriate attitude will be evident in one's manner of presiding in liturgy as well as in one's teaching and pastoral work in general. In fact, the body language of rite often communicates attitudes more effectively than verbal expression. Even the hint of a swagger or of proprietorship or of exclusive sources of inspiration is devastating to one's service as a presider. A profound consciousness of the common human potential for grace and the transformation wrought by faith and initiation is no doubt the reason why the earliest generations of Christians avoided sacerdotal terminology except when speaking of Christ and why the church employed it again only when it could be reinterpreted in the established light of our common baptismal dignity.

Socioeconomic Responsibilities of the Local Church. Consequently, according to articles 7–17, initiation and its sacraments are the business of the entire local church, not merely the business of the clergy. The presiding role now can be understood and appropriately performed only by one who is conscious at every moment that the whole faith community is the basis of and is represented in everything the presider does. Specialized ministries are *not* private and individual powers.

One can understand why, given the ecclesiologies and notions of ministry prevalent in the past several centuries, people will invite clergy with no relation to the local church, but with ties of friendship or relation to the parties most intimately involved, to preside at liturgies of baptism, marriage, death and other special occasions. With an improved and postconciliar ecclesiology, however, that custom makes no sense at all. These liturgies, like others, are always celebrations of the local church, not merely of the parties being baptized, married or laid to rest. What one looks for, then, is not a presider after one's heart or to one's taste, but rather the locus of the Sunday assembly for the people involved, the church whose worship and mission the relevant parties have shared. The local church is the celebrant, the actor, the critical element—not the presiding minister who represents that community and, therefore, Christ.

The Paschal and Social Character of Baptism. According to articles 18–29, everything within the power of the presider's teaching and example must be done to emphasize the "paschal character" (28), as well as the social and community character of baptism and the variety of specialized ministries appropriate in its celebration. The most suitable day for baptisms is Easter and the most suitable liturgy is the Easter Vigil, whether it is conducted at dawn or midnight.

Previous emphasis on the baptism of infants soon after birth must yield to these characteristics as well as to the pastoral necessity of preparing parents and godparents through instruction. At the very least, baptism should be celebrated in a principal liturgy of the local church and "as far as possible, all recently born babies should be baptized at a common celebration on the same day" (27).

Since the invention of the printing press, our obsession with liturgical books and words has made most of us poor presiders, dulling us to the power of the visual and other sense experiences in rite. While immersion is not required, it is "more suitable" (22). Like the opening up of other sacramental actions and objects, the immersion of children or adults in fonts constructed for these purposes (or portable) is a central and critical part of liturgical renewal. Presiders should take the lead in the advocacy and practice of immersion, not only because it is recommended by the liturgical books, but also because it communicates the meaning of initiation much more effectively than any other method. Immersion is like most of the nonverbals in our liturgical tradition. One can talk about immersion forever without progress, but one experience of participating in that act resolves all doubts.

Christian Initiation of Adults: Introduction

The presider as cleric formerly functioned as practically the sole mouthpiece of the faith community in the process of welcoming and instructing newcomers. Now according to RCIA, 4, the presider must take special pains to involve as many members of the local church as possible not only in the training part of this new process but also in the rites that mark and celebrate its steps. "The initiation is a gradual process that takes place step by step in the midst of the community of the faithful" (4).

This may be particularly important at first, when the local church is not yet well established in the pattern and practice of RCIA. As pastoral leader—or one of them—in the community, the presider cannot merely hope that the other members of the staff and the congregation as a whole will assume these new responsibilities. Preaching, teaching, scheduling initiation rites for principal assemblies of the church, structuring both training and rites to involve as many in the parish as possible—all the tools at the presider's command—will have to be employed. A catechumenate is a revolutionary change in the life of the local church. While it may take many years and perhaps generations to make it second nature to all of us, the beginning steps are crucial.

The presider must realize that it is the vast majority in our parishes who need what initiation offers, not merely the inquirers or catechumens. Even though baptism is never repeated, the initiation process is in a sense the very structure of the Christian life and of the liturgical year. It is repeated over and over again.

According to RCIA, 3, part of the collegial consciousness of a good presider is the awareness of our need of one another's insights and approaches to faith in the process of growing up in Christ. Together we are Christ's body. None of us is the whole Christ. The church's teaching authority is a pastoral function, which is to say that the chief pastors or bishops are assumed to be in close contact with what the Spirit is doing in all parts of the church and in all its members.

Scripture says, "As one face differs from another, so does one human heart from another."[4] This article points out that the "spiritual journey of adults . . . varies according to the many forms of God's grace." A presider in a local church, then, assumes a pastoral role that requires attention and listening to new members and veterans, young and old, both sexes, all types and kinds.

Familiarity gained by experience with the four periods of "investigation and maturation" will see this process become an umbrella under which virtually all of the activities of a local church are gathered: liturgy, adult education, sacramental preparation, corporate witness and administration. In other words, the initiation process becomes in time the *structure* of parish life as the result of a natural, unforced development.

The relationship between the other activities of these periods and their initiating or climactic rites teaches the sensitive presider something about the pastoral function. This function has been much obscured by our current tendency to an almost constant presbyteral ritualizing. Presiding in liturgy does not exhaust the pastoral role but, rather, it is its climax. The pastor's job is to work with the members of the church: building a faith community capable of celebrating, eliciting their gifts, strengthening their bonds with one another, enabling their service to the rest of the world as a sign of God's reign. All specialized ministers in the church have work to do that precedes any liturgical roles that they might have. To be confined almost exclusively to these roles is to leave the real world and to make one's home in an impotent clerical ghetto.

If one looks merely at the liturgical rites that mark the steps or stages of the initiation process, one misses the point. The rites celebrate something that has been going on outside the rites. Similarly, if one looks merely at the rite of the Sunday assembly and its presider, one misses the point. For that eucharist, also, celebrates something that has been going on outside and before the rite.

According to RCIA, 9, "The people of God, as represented by the local church, should understand and show by their concern that the initiation of adults is the responsibility of all the baptized," including children. This article simply emphasizes the comments that already have been made, stressing that the presider's role involves not only a kind of choreography of the whole community's participation in the initiation process but also an organizing direction of the variety of other roles of specialized ministry appropriate both to the process and to its rites: deacons, catechists/readers, sponsors/godparents and the rest.

According to RCIA, 13, the presider "is to be diligent in the correct celebration and adaptation of the rites throughout the entire rite of Christian initiation." The liturgy (Bible and sacrament) is the primary and indispensable source, and all else in this process must be related organically to that fundamental formation. The liturgy is where our basics are at. When we have our feet planted firmly on that ground, we can grow up and become adult Christians with consciences, no longer dependent on our little lists of do's and don'ts.

Good presiders, for example, do not depart from the readings and the signs of the times in preaching. While this is a general rule for all liturgy, it is a critical requirement in relation to the catechumenate. If catechumens and other members of the local church are encouraged by this kind of preaching to be Bible readers in their private prayer life, this alone would make the initiation process invaluable.

Even though newcomers learn to pray by participating in appropriate liturgical rites and by more informal prayer in other groups where old-timers and newcomers pray together, the presider offers a particularly powerful example. Whether in formal services or at other meetings, the presider's extemporaneous prayers should be carefully prepared and scriptural-liturgical in their inspiration and form (clearly God-centered, addressed to God through Christ and in the Spirit, observing the primacy of thanks and praise, avoiding length and pedantry). Because the presider's task is to personify or embody in that function the entire local church, the whole faith community—women and men, old and young, minority as well as majority ethnic groups, gay and straight, sick and healthy, "normal" and handicapped—one must insist that the presider take special care that all language in the church, especially the language of public prayer, be freed by artful adaptation from sexism and racism and other prejudices of our past.

Finally, the kind of presider desired by RCIA (and therefore by the church at its deepest and best everywhere and always) is a person keenly aware of the limits of words and verbal formulas, a person appreciative and enthusiastic concerning the incomparable communication of liturgy's nonverbal elements. Symbolic act, music, body language, sensations of sight, sound, touch, smell, taste—these elements of liturgical tradition, when they are not cramped and minimized, when they are used joyfully and richly and fully, speak a language that is foreign to no one and immensely more meaningful than verbal tongues. Nowhere is that potent language more important and necessary than before the inscrutable mystery of God.

♦ *Robert W. Hovda*

Notes

1. Cyrille Vogel, "An Alienated Liturgy," *Liturgy: Self-Expression of the Church*, edited by Herman Schmidt, SJ (New York: Herder & Herder, 1972), 19.

2. "General Introduction" to "Christian Initiation" of the *Roman Ritual* and "Introduction" to the *Rite of Christian Initiation of Adults*, translations of both were emended by the International Commission on English in the Liturgy (ICEL) to accord with the Code of Canon Law of 1983 and the adaptational needs of national conferences of Catholic bishops in the English-speaking world, the emendation of the former issued in 1983 by the Congregation for Divine Worship, and the emendation of the latter confirmed for use in the United States of America by the Apostolic See on 19 February 1988; see *Rite of Christian Initiation of Adults* (Chicago IL: Liturgy Training Publications), xiv-xviii; 2-12.

3. Peter Fink, SJ, "The Sacrament of Orders: Some Liturgical Reflections," *Worship* 56 (1982), 485.

4. Proverbs 27:19.

What Kind of Lenten Homilies Does the Catechumenate Want?

OOD HOMILIES? Well-prepared homilies? Interesting and well-delivered homilies? These and like responses clearly beg the question posed above. Lenten preaching—particularly in assemblies where the elect and catechumens[1] are celebrating the Sunday liturgy of the word with the faithful—is burdened and blessed by special responsibilities above and beyond those that belong to the homilist during the normal course of events. The presupposition in the title assigned for this chapter is that the Rite of Christian Initiation of Adults (RCIA) looks for some particular brand of preaching, the likes of which may be either unnecessary or unwarranted at other times during the course of the liturgical year. Such presupposing is not without merit and is deserving of our attention before attempting to answer the title question.

The Homily on Ordinary Sundays

Occasionally on a Sunday there is a temptation to preach a sermon rather than a homily, to moralize rather than proclaim the good news, to run a film rather than use a live human voice or even to race from gospel to creed with no reflection at all.

By means of the homily the mysteries of the faith and the guiding principles of the Christian life are expounded from the sacred text during the course of the liturgical year; *as part of the liturgy itself*, therefore, the homily is strongly recommended. (*Constitution on the Sacred Liturgy*, 52)[2]

During the 25 years since these words first were published, has the homily come to be understood as part of the liturgy itself? Has it in fact come to *be* a part of that liturgy? As a rule, at most Sunday Masses the proclamation of the gospel is followed by some form of preaching. For better or for worse, on target or missing the mark by a mile, someone usually gets up between the people's "Praise to you, Lord Jesus Christ!" and the creed to speak in a homiletic vein. But the demand of the *Constitution on the Sacred Liturgy* is that the homily be not only a regular feature in our celebration of the eucharist but also an *integral* element of that liturgical act.

While we readily would identify the entrance rites, the collects, the eucharistic prayer and the communion processional as parts of the liturgy, we may be slower to appreciate the homily as belonging to the liturgy in quite the same way. For many, the homily still is understood to stand somehow apart or distinct from the other texts and actions that constitute our liturgical prayer. Preachers who still begin and end their homilies by making the sign of the cross are ritualizing this ill-advised thinking.

It may seem to some that only the given, official texts are the *real* texts of our ritual and that the homily is an extraneous (even if sometimes helpful and complementary) addition. And because it is *additional*, it is also dispensable. Few pastors would drop the giving of the parish announcements during the heat of summer, but many feel that higher humidity and vacation schedules are sufficient reasons for suspending the preaching of God's word during July and August.

As the proclamation of the gospel and the offering of the eucharistic prayer are parts of the liturgy, so too is the homily a part of the liturgy itself. "It flows from the scriptures, which are read at the liturgical celebration or, more broadly, from the scriptures that undergird its prayers and actions, and it enables the congregation to participate in the celebration with faith."[3]

Indeed, the homily is the bridge over which the assembly of God's people pass from the table of the word to the table of the eucharist. "In the eucharistic celebration the homily points to the presence of God in people's lives and then leads a congregation into the eucharist, providing, as it were, the motive for celebrating the eucharist in this time and place."[4] The homily should break open the scriptures for us in such a way that we are impelled toward the altar of praise and thanksgiving.

The good homily is an interpretation of the word proclaimed in light of our experience of life and an interpretation of our experience of life in light of the word proclaimed—all for the purpose of stirring our hearts to praise and thanksgiving for God's saving love. This is our "duty and our salvation," always and everywhere to give thanks to God through Jesus Christ. The good homily, then, tells us less about how we should live and more about where we should go: to the Lord's table!

The members of our Sunday assemblies know this; they sense it. How can we otherwise account for the fact that those who have little or no training in the liturgical arts and sciences so accurately pinpoint the failure of preaching as a critical issue in the life of the community's prayer? It is not so much that poor preaching leaves people bored—though indeed it does. Worse yet, it leaves them hungry! Our people hunger for the food that is knowledge of God and discernment of how God moves in our lives. Our people hunger for the word and hunger for the nourishment of the sacramental table, access to which is at least inhibited, if not sometimes spiritually prohibited, when the homily fails to serve as a warm invitation to the praise and thanksgiving of the eucharist.

We rehearse all of this not because it is new, but because it is something that we often forget in preparing for liturgical celebrations in general and in preparing for homilies in particular. Understanding the homily as an entity that is *integral* to the whole liturgical action is always important, but it is perhaps at no time during the course of the liturgical year *more* important than during Lent, particularly in those assemblies blessed by the presence of both elect and catechumens. It celebrates Christ's real presence in word, eucharist, ministers and assembly.

The Season of Lent:
The Context of Our Ritual Prayer

Lent is the annual retreat for the assembly of believers. It is spring training for Christians: a time to tone up, a time to strengthen what has grown weak, a time to trim away excess, a time to practice the basic skills of the Christian life through prayer, fasting and almsgiving. Lent is preparation for the season of new life that the community enters when it celebrates the Easter mysteries. Lent is a time to live for a season the life that Christians are called to live every day.

Lent is frequently a time of heightened sensitivity in the community. Faithful members are making an effort to be more faithful to word, sacrament and the works of justice. Those who are not so faithful may come home on Ash Wednesday and try to renew their membership in the life of Christ's body, the church. Many are searching their souls, taking inventory: acknowledging, naming and confessing their brokenness. They hope to be healed, restored and forgiven. Indeed, it is a time when more ears and more hearts are open to hear God's word as it is proclaimed and broken open for our nourishment. It is a time when hearts are ready to hear the calls for repentance and conversion.

Because this greater openness may render the assembly receptive to hearing the word proclaimed and preached, it increases the preacher's burdens and responsibilities. When the hearts of many are open to the sound and touch and power of God's word, those who preach must be particularly articulate, especially sensitive and genuinely convicted by the word entrusted to them on behalf of God's people. It goes without saying, of course, that the preacher's own heart, in like fashion, is prepared to be healed, having been readied by the prayer, fasting and almsgiving to which the gospel calls those on both sides of the ambo.

And as if all this were not enough, into our Sunday assembly troops a band of men and women seeking communion in our society of redeemed sinners. Enter the catechumens and the elect!

The Catechumens and the Elect

The catechumenate is the Lord's way of keeping the church honest. Through the catechumenate we admit to the intimacy of our Sunday assembly people whose presence challenges who we are and how we live as the body of Christ. Here are men and women whose inquiring and beautifully naive faith comes face-to-face with the "faith of the faithful" that may have grown dull or jaded. We enroll those who come with honest and difficult questions for which, we may be embarrassed to admit, we have no ready response. We welcome those whose presence is a mirror in which we, the baptized, see ourselves for who we are. The catechumens and the elect bring us up short. Their presence calls our bluff. Their dismissal before the general intercessions reminds us weekly of the deep truth of our prayer: "Lord, I am not worthy to receive you, but only say the word and I shall be healed."

The lenten community is truly incomplete without the catechumens and the elect. They are an integral part of our observance of Lent-Easter-Pentecost. They are living sacraments, *signs* of the mysteries we celebrate. These men and women are an image for us in a unique way of the powerful movement of God's word and Spirit in the hearts of the faithful. Nothing can equal the power of this group whose journey we are invited to share. The final weeks of lenten preparation are especially important for those seeking a share in the communion that is already ours with the Lord and with one another.

If Lent is spring training for Christians, then the catechumens and the elect are, without knowing it, the trainers. Even in their absence after the dismissal, they call us to that cleansing scrutiny of our lives that the prayer and penance of Lent is intended to achieve. Those who come seeking initiation become the models for the initiated. With the catechumens' passage from inquiry to enrollment, we learn to ponder again what we once faithfully treasured and what we may have come to take for granted. At their election we are confronted with the office that we hold: with our fidelity and our infidelity as the servants of God. In scrutinizing the elect, we confront the power of evil in our own lives and confess again our deliverance from sin through the power of God.

What Kind of Homilies?

There is in all of this a great and wonderful convergence of people of faith and of their journeys, of the season of purple and of its prayer and ritual. The homily's role in all of this is so much more than simply naming or pointing out or (worse yet) *explaining* the convergence. Such preaching stands apart from the liturgy and may be little more than a peripheral instruction on the ritual action. The very meaning and function of the homily is determined by its relation to the liturgical action of which it is a part. The homily on a Sunday in Lent must function as an integral *part* of the liturgy: It is meant to be a *piece* of the action—not a commentary on it. What kind of homilies, then, does the catechumenate want?

Homilies Flow from Scripture. The catechumenate wants homilies that are rooted in the living word of God, homilies that flow from the scriptures. The presumption here is that the liturgy of the word up to the homily, in particular the proclamation of the readings, has been a living, flowing event, out of which some nourishing, substantial homily reasonably might issue. If the scriptures are merely read, mumbled or recited, the homilist's work is already severely sabotaged. There is neither time nor place in the homily for summarizing the readings when their proclamation has failed to communicate the Lord's word. The preacher depends on the readers, and rightly so, to proclaim a significant part of the liturgy. We might even say that the proclamation of the scriptures is the first part of the homily: The homilist picks up where the scriptures (and those who proclaim them) have left off.

As the scriptures clearly tell how God's redeeming life and presence have been woven into the fabric of the lives of the chosen, so the homilist picks up the strands of yarn and tells how the life and presence of the same Lord continues to weave itself in our stories and our times. The catechumenate wants a homilist, then, who knows the story of salvation as it is told in the scriptures, a homilist who loves that story and who loves to *tell* that story, a homilist who knows the stories of the community of believers who have gathered around the table of the word to be fed. The homilist who does not know the story of the local church and the stories of the catechumens cannot preach a welcome to those who come knocking at the door seeking membership in that church. Such a homilist holds only the strands of the scriptures in hand and at best might guess at the texture and strength of the lives of those seeking to be woven into the fabric of the community's faith.

The storytelling here is nothing less than a matter of salvation: We are talking about people's lives, the life of the church, the lives of its members and of those who seek communion with us. "Unless a preacher knows what a congregation needs, wants or is able to hear, there is every possibility that the message offered in the homily will not meet the needs of the people who hear it."[5] We cannot be content with preachers who know only the punch lines: What the catechumenate wants and what the church needs are preachers who know the whole story and the stories behind the story. The catechumenate wants the preaching of a homilist who knows the personal stories that will give shape, content and depth to the ritual's script.

Ritual Actions Flow from Homilies. The catechumenate wants homilies from which the ritual actions freely flow. As the homily on most Sundays is meant to invite the assembly to the table of the eucharist, so on those days when the rites for catechumens and the elect are celebrated, the homily serves to bring us first to the particular ritual (after which the catechumens are dismissed) and then to the table of the sacrament.

What this requires of the homilist is deep appreciation for the catechumenate as a whole and for the rite being celebrated in particular. Only those who have come to understand the conversion dynamic of the catechumenate and understand its implications for parish life should step to the ambo to preach on the occasion of the celebration of these rites. Those who still confuse the rite of becoming a catechumen with the rite of enrollment have no business preaching before either rite is celebrated. The litmus test for readiness is how well the potential preacher understands the scrutinies! Degrees in liturgy are not required here, only a healthy grasp of the rites: their shape and form, their function and meaning.

Just as the homilist does not *explain* the scriptures but rather offers an interpretation of them for our own experience, so the homilist on these days does not explain the rite about to be conducted but preaches in such a way that performing the rite leads to an enfleshment of the message preached. What is needed here is a *flow* between the proclamation of the scriptures, the homily and the celebration of the rite. Explanations and play-by-play commentaries interrupt this flow.

Words for the Faithful. The catechumenate wants homilies that speak to people of faith. "The fact that the homily is addressed to a congregation of believers who have gathered to worship indicates that its purpose is not conversion from radical unbelief to belief. Nor does the homily primarily concern itself with a systematic theological understanding of faith. A homily presupposes faith. It is preached in order that a community of believers who have gathered to celebrate the liturgy may do so more deeply and more fully— more faithfully—and thus be formed for Christian witness in the world."[6]

Those who belong to the order of catechumens and those who are the elect are people of faith. "You have sought and summoned them in many ways and they have turned to seek you. You have called them today and they have answered in our presence." (RCIA, 53) "They have received the sign of their new way of life in being signed with the cross of Jesus Christ." (RCIA, 54) "They have been entrusted with the book of the gospels." (RCIA, 64) "They have listened to the word of Christ and endeavored to follow his commands; they have shared the company of their Christian brothers and sisters and joined with them in prayer." (RCIA, 131) The homilist serves only embarrassment by preaching as though the catechumens are strangers to the faith of the gospel. The community of the baptized faithful that enfolds the elect and the catechumens in its embrace needs to hear its own faith articulated, challenged, nurtured, cajoled and urged toward growth and depth. It is never the homilist's task on any Sunday to instill faith in the assembly, much less on the Sundays of Lent when the faithful's attention to God's word is particularly acute and attuned. The catechumenate wants homilies that are honest. The members of the assembly best respond when they are addressed as who they are: people of faith!

The Catechumenate and Homilies

Because this author is unfamiliar with the stories of the readers' communities and their catechumens, it would not be helpful at this point to offer homiletic suggestions. Instead, and in keeping with all that has been said above, I offer a format or structure to assist the preacher in preparing homilies for the rite of election, the scrutinies and the presentations of the creed and the Lord's Prayer.

Begin with the Scriptures. All good liturgical preparation begins with the scripture texts for the liturgy at hand: There is no other legitimate place to begin. Listen for the *story* in the gospel and listen for its echo in the other two readings. Stay with the story until you get it—until you understand its contents, characters, message, subtleties and intent. What is the Lord speaking here? What is the challenge? What is the comfort of this piece of the good news? Where and how—names, faces, places, circumstances, events, memories—do these scriptures reverberate in the hearts and in the structures of the community who will celebrate with these texts?

Consider the Context of the Season. Lent is the church's annual, solemn retreat, marked by penance and preparation for initiation. How does the purple of Lent and longed-for white and yellow and gold of Easter baptism color our understanding of these scriptures? What is the difference in preaching on the story of the transfiguration on August 6 and on the second Sunday of Lent? What is the relationship of these scriptures to the church's lenten discipline, to this community's practice of discipline and to the presence of the catechumens within the community and its worship: names, faces, places, circumstances, events, memories? How do these texts relate to our preparation for the annual celebration of the Lord's paschal mystery?

Consider the Catechumenal Rite for the Day. In the rite of enrollment or election, the scrutinies, the presentation of the creed and Lord's Prayer, what are the ritual actions? What shape, form and content do the participants give to the ritual action? How does the life and story of this community provide the context for this ritual action? How do the lives and stories of the elect and catechumens incarnate what the ritual actions signify? What are the words that accompany the action? How do these words and actions relate to the community's worship and life, particularly in the season of Lent? How do the day's scripture lessons prepare the community for the celebration of this rite?

And consider the rite in the context of the community's worship. As important as they are, the rites most often are not our principal reason for gathering. In most instances the rites are celebrated at Sunday Mass: The community has gathered to be nourished by God's word and by the eucharist. Even for the elect and the catechumens who are dismissed after the celebration of the rite, all is not at an end: They are dismissed to continue their study of the word. The homily that focuses entirely on the rite will be a homily that is out of focus with the community's prayer and the rhythms of its larger liturgical context.

Tell a Ten-Year-Old. Having heard the scriptures through the ears of your community's heart and life, having heard the scriptures through the filter of the liturgical season, having understood the rite in relationship to the people hearing this word and celebrating this season, now formulate how you might communicate all of this to a ten-year-old in about five minutes. (How much time do you think a ten-year-old would give you?) This exercise keeps the homilist honest, to the point and faithful to what is really important. This is not to suggest that one preach to the assembly as though they were a class of fourth-graders but rather to indicate that the preacher who can simply and honestly communicate all this to a child is ready to expand the content and style and to preach to a parish community—which usually includes ten-year-olds—the kind of homily that the catechumenate wants.

◆ *Austin H. Fleming*

Notes

1. The presumption in this chapter is that in many, if not most, communities the catechumens and elect will be present for the liturgy of the word on the Sundays of Lent.

2. See also *Fulfilled in Your Hearing: The Homily in the Sunday Assembly,* issued by the Bishops' Committee on Priestly Life and Ministry (Washington DC: United States Catholic Conference, 1981), 17.

3. Ibid., 23.

4. Eucharistic Prayer for Mass of Reconciliation 1.

5. *Fulfilled in Your Hearing*, 4.

6. Ibid., 17–18.

Suggestions for Further Reading

Burghardt, Walter J., SJ *Lovely in Eyes Not His: Homilies for an Imaging of Christ* (New York: Paulist Press, 1988).

————— , *Preaching: The Art and the Craft* (New York: Paulist Press, 1987).

Christian Initiation of Adults: A Commentary, Study Text 10 (Washington DC: Office of Publishing and Promotion Services, United States Catholic Conference, 1985).

Huck, Gabe, "The Third, Fourth and Fifth Sundays of Lent," *Liturgy 80* (January 1988), 9.

McMahon, J. Michael, *The Rite of Christian Initiation of Adults* (Washington DC: Federation of Diocesan Liturgical Commissions, 1986).

Searle, Mark, "For the Glory of God: The Scrutiny for the Fifth Sunday of Lent," *Catechumenate: A Journal of Christian Initiation* (November 1987), 2–11.

What Kind of Eastertime Homilies Does the Catechumenate Want?

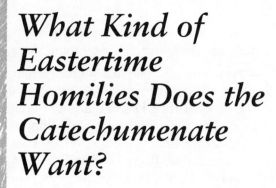

P

REACHING RECEIVES much criticism in current surveys and statistics. Faults and failings are quickly and frequently noted. The good news behind the bad news is simply that assemblies seek to hear good preaching because they seek the nourishment of the word made flesh.

The paradox here for Catholics, again good news, is that the liturgy of the word has been rediscovered. Perhaps it is part of the informational age, perhaps it is because of the participatory nature of the word compared to the (so far) passive nature of the eucharistic prayer, perhaps it is simply the work of the Spirit.

Both the criticism and the challenge of preaching include several issues. Many, if not all, of these issues come to the surface during Eastertime and, in so doing, present an excellent opportunity for attention in an integral and nourishing way for both preacher and assembly. While parish liturgy commissions and professional liturgists struggle to keep Eastertime alive, preachers who can call on experiences within the Rite of Christian Initiation of Adults (RCIA) will be able to fulfill the expectations and demands of the homily and of the season.

Contemporary criticisms of preaching, both from the preacher's and the assembly's viewpoint, include the following:

— Preaching is too often a simple retelling of the gospel story, leaving the listener not in the contemporary world but in ancient history, hearing tales of miracles and visions from another time and place. Preaching, so we hear, seldom relates to the lives of the present assembly, the bread-and-butter issues. Is the Lord and the power of the Spirit alive and well now, or must one seek out a more charismatic experience and maybe another church?

— When the homily *is* upbeat, optimistic and filled with good news, both preachers and parishioners complain that there is too little teaching about the commandments, the cost of discipleship, the role of suffering in the lives of Christians. In a consumer society marked by severe individualism, is there nothing to call listeners to a sense of responsibility and ministry? Who will invite us to gather, live and serve as church?

— An important newcomer to the list is the growing concern, aptly described by Elisabeth Schüssler Fiorenza, that even the best homily normally reflects only one person's experience and faith expression. Usually that person is male and celibate.[1]

This list is not to suggest a program of topics to be dutifully covered in a mystagogia lecture series to neophytes. It simply reveals the dynamics available within the Fifty Days of Easter. Community, church and commandments, as well as contemporary adult experiences of the sacraments and the possibility or presence of the cost of conversion, all are a part of this season.

Assembly Benefits from Catechumenal Presence

Certainly many of the subjects have been treated—and experienced—in catechumenal gatherings with catechists and sponsors. The congregation has witnessed the dismissal of the catechumens for many months and has participated with those same catechumens in rites of acceptance, anointing, presentation of the creed and Lord's Prayer, scrutinies and exorcisms, in addition to any social or ministerial functions that may have brought them together. In some parishes, however, there is still a separateness between catechumens and the assembly. Some members of the assembly may have the impression that at Eastertime catechumens come from their basement meeting rooms to reveal that something has happened, a perception that needs appropriate information and clarification from the pastoral staff, catechumenate team and catechists. With suitable catechesis, incomplete or mistaken impressions like this so easily can reawaken the word broken open among the entire assembly.

The church Fathers, known for their poetic mystagogical sermons, experienced adult sacramental circumstances as reference points. For us it is difficult to remember personal and significant experiences of conversion or the initiation sacraments. The presence of adults who have experienced both the joys and struggles of conversion and the tangible realities of rich sacramental symbols provides both preacher and assembly with a rich resource for a nourishing experience of the word.

Walter Burghardt discusses how imagination functions in preaching to "make present and active the mystery of Christ." Indoctrination plays upon one faculty of the human person: the intellect's ability to grasp ideas, concepts, propositions. It pays little heed to an old scholastic axiom, "Nothing is present in the intellect that was not previously present in the senses." Our ideas are triggered by sense experience. The more powerful the sense experience, the more powerfully an idea will take hold. If I want to sell you on Spaghetti Bolognese or Beef Burgundy, I don't hand you a recipe; I let you smell it, taste it, savor it.[2]

During Eastertime, the parish with an active catechumenate has more than Beef Burgundy, even more than a handy visual aid for a homiletic point. With the neophytes, it has in its presence a lived experience of the saving mystery. The lectionary selections from the Acts of the Apostles during Eastertime provide evidence that the early church did more than tell stories about Jesus who died and rose. Rather, in their paschal liturgies the members of that church experienced within their own time the very life of the risen Christ and the imitation of his earthly journey.

This focus on the experience of the church is so integral to the season that any preacher attempting to speak only of the *historical* Jesus or present only his *teachings* will be hard-pressed to find support in the biblical text. For some individuals baptism may precede the experience of the Spirit, but for some others the experience of the Spirit's presence is evident earlier and calls for baptism.

Should Neophytes Bear Witness from the Pulpit?

The readings of Eastertime, together with the experience of the neophytes and the community, provide more than enough material for a homily. They are sacramental moments—ancient words joined to present events reveal God's presence: *"Accedit verbum ad elementum et fit sacramentum"* (St. Augustine). As the presider must be united with the church for this to happen in eucharist, so, too, the preacher must be in touch with the experiences of the neophytes and alert to the comments of the community as well. Listening to his own and others' experiences, not only of the Vigil but of conversion itself, its joys and its difficulties, is essential to the Eastertime homiletic process.

The decision to have the preacher reflect such experiences in the homily or actually have neophytes tell their own story is a pastorally sensitive one. In either case, as with any personal story employed in preaching, the purpose is not to draw attention to oneself but to serve as a mirror or sacrament in which the community can see beyond the individual to the working of grace and discover a reflection of a similar grace in their own lives.

In choosing to have the neophytes speak, it should be noted that their purpose is not to give a homily. Rather, they provide a certain witness; they tell the story of what it has meant to join this particular community. With honesty and discretion, they describe their prayer, their enlightenment and even the possible struggle and rejection involved in their conversion. The lectionary selections expand on these themes during this season. Such testimony probably would be brief and combined with others, lest one person be singled out.

Nor is such witnessing limited to the new members. One dynamic of the season is certainly the experience of conversion or joining as a way to renew the faith of many in the assembly. More traditionally, however, mystagogy is the church itself setting the fullness of the gospel and the sacramental life before the neophytes and the whole assembly. The Easter readings remind all of the role of the commandments, the struggle not to conform to the world, and the call to service. A preacher addressing such topics will be speaking to new and old members alike. Moreover, following the model of witnessing, members of the assembly might prepare their own brief stories, focusing either on the joys and struggles of Christian life or the experience of Christian ministry. This would be preferable to simply announcing the various organizations available for the new members to join.

may not be applicable in all situations. Pastoral sensitivity to the needs of the whole assembly is required. Some people in the assembly, because of their ignorance, their reluctance to make the proper distinctions or simply their inability to accept change as readily as others can, may object to what they still would call "lay preaching." As an alternative or simply as weekly policy in the parish, the following practice works well and is always recommended. When the homilist gathers with others from the parish to prepare the Sunday homily, marvelous things can happen. One finds this practice in many parishes. Where this has yet to be tried, Eastertime may provide the best opportunity and the best experience. Obviously, the more the preacher has been involved in the catechumenate, the richer will be the experience of the exchange and the story that results.

The Eastertime Sunday Lectionary

A simple review of the readings of Eastertime provides the basis and focus for much of what is important for liturgies during this season. The following, drawn from just a few of the Sundays, is not intended as a list of topics but rather an attempt to identify some of the dynamics within the readings. May they provide a beginning for your own discovery.

The Second Sunday of Easter, featuring the story of the doubting Thomas in all three cycles, presents the words: "Blest are they who have not seen and believed." Surely the reference is to the church itself, to us and especially those who have listened to the words recorded "so that through this faith you may have life in his name." The first reading of the Second Sunday, in Cycles A and B, speaks of the early church, its growing numbers and its life of interdependence and concern for the poor. Certainly we have here not only a reflection of our present experience of growth but a challenge to support each other in spiritual and temporal needs, as well as to respond to the needs of the poor. How often the complaint is heard that we are a church of strangers that only modestly responds to the poor! How quickly the newly baptized and new members are lost in the vast numbers and independent lives within our parishes!

The second reading of this same Sunday in Cycle A again speaks of those who believe without seeing, as well as the joy and the suffering of the disciples' present life. The Cycle B selection from John speaks of commandments but also provides the source of living the commandments, the One who came through water and blood, two rich sacramental symbols. And for those attempting to deal with the visions of John in the second reading of Cycle C, remember that neophytes often have imaginative ways of referring to their discovery of the Lord.

As with so many of the resurrection accounts, the Third Sunday of Easter, Cycle A, provides the setting of a meal for the encounter with the risen Lord. The Emmaus story brilliantly reflects the two dynamics of the liturgy: word and sacrament. It may become an invitation for others to provide contemporary evidence of hearts that have been inflamed by scripture and ways in which both new and old members have found the presence of the Lord in the breaking of the bread.

The gospel reading from Cycle C for this same Sunday again presents a meal and adds to it the mandate to feed others as well as the caution that one may be led in surprising ways. Older members of the community frequently have stories of where faith has taken them.

The second reading on the Fourth Sunday, Cycle B, provides an opportunity to speak of suffering, not simply in general, but suffering from doing good. Likewise, the first readings in Cycle C on the Third, Fourth and Fifth Sundays and the second readings in Cycle A on the Sixth and Seventh Sundays include passages on the cost of discipleship. They remind the listeners that rejection may be part of the Christian life. Examples both from the tradition of the church as well as contemporary stories and examples from our own community, sensitively chosen, might prove helpful in presenting the church as prophet, questioning the ways of the world and standing against dishonesty and injustice in whatever forms they may arise.

As with the catechumenate period itself, there need not be a feeling of urgency that all is covered in this season or this year. Remember that our bishops are requesting that the mystagogical program for neophytes be a year in length (see the National Statutes for the Catechumenate, 24).

What I have suggested and encouraged here is simply that the preparation and preaching of the homily during Eastertime reflect a saving moment, not simply satisfying ideas. Such is possible if the preacher focuses one eye on the readings of Eastertime and the traditions and current experience of the universal church and the other eye on the lived experiences of both the new and the old members of the community.

♦ *James T. Telthorst*

Notes

1. As noted in Walter J. Burghardt, SJ, *Preaching: The Art and the Craft* (New York: Paulist Press, 1987), 68–70.

2. Ibid., 23.

What Kind of Process Does the Catechumenate Want?

A S THE POST-VATICAN II years turn into decades, countless attempts continue to be made to discover not only the meaning but also the implications of a church defined as "the people of God" (*Dogmatic Constitution on the Church*, chapter 2). My own development of a philosophy of Shared Wisdom is one of those attempts. In this chapter, I will summarize my philosophy and then offer some practical implications for its use in the catechumenate experience.

The Philosophy of Shared Wisdom

Jesus speaks clearly to us in the Gospel of Matthew when he tells us that whenever we gather he will be with us (Matthew 18:20) and then promises: "Behold, I am with you always" (Matthew 28:20). These statements define us as believers, as Christians, as church. We are the presence of the risen Lord for one another!

Through baptism the Spirit dwells within us. Through baptism we become church. Through baptism we are called to ministry.

Through baptism we become the people of God. We are, therefore, the church of the baptized. Or, to say it another way, the responsibility to be church, to form and nourish church, belongs not only to the ordained but to the baptized. We all can take on that responsibility precisely because of the presence of the incarnate God. Incarnation is not just something that happened two thousand years ago. The word continues to be made flesh in our lives. Scripture continues to be written through our life stories. As the Spirit came upon Mary and allowed her to give birth to the word of God, so the Spirit impregnates us to allow the word to live and to be present in our world.

Let me say it another way: Each of us, through our lived experience, has a "piece of the wisdom." The Spirit, who impregnates us, who walks the journeys of life with us, also shares wisdom with us. This, of course, does not make us all instant experts on everything. It is important to remember that we each have only "a piece." No one but God has all the pieces. That also means that we have different pieces depending on our life experiences and our efforts to be in touch with the God of those experiences.

The philosophy of Shared Wisdom flows from this understanding of incarnational theology. To the degree that any group will gather all the pieces and allow them to impact on each other, to that degree they will arrive at the will of the Spirit for that group.

Is it possible to misinterpret or completely miss the wisdom of the Spirit? Indeed it is! A Shared Wisdom model of parish, community, diocese, council, board or staff calls for a commitment to a personal spirituality that will foster each person's awareness of the action of the Spirit in the experiences of the daily journey. Only as each person comes to trust the God of his or her lived experience will he or she be able to trust the God of the gathering present in the diocese, the parish, the council, the catechumenate.

The Church into Which We Invite Catechumens

A Vatican II parish is a parish in which all the people of God are valued and treasured. It is a parish where pastor, staff and parishioners are in process. It is a parish where laity, religious and clergy are learning to share responsibility for the life of the parish. It is a parish where laity, religious and clergy are moving into appropriate mutuality in liturgical ritual and decision making. It is a parish where laity, religious and clergy are increasingly committed to their own personal spiritual growth and are learning how to assist one another on the journey toward spiritual wholeness. It is a parish where the issues of human rights, world peace and concern for the poor and marginal are recognized as the right to life's "seamless garment."

Is it a perfect parish? Of course not! No such parish exists. But it is "on the way." There is evidence of mutual respect, a recognition that no one really knows how "to do" church but that all contribute to the learning process: the direct result of the call of Vatican II.

This model of church needs to be experienced by the catechumens. It is healthy and honest for the catechumens to see the struggles, the efforts, the sincerity, the fear, the hope, the questions, the doubts that accompany the efforts of the laity to be involved in councils, boards, commissions and committees. It is healthy, too, for them to be made aware of the problems inherent in the new models as clergy and religious struggle to give up and share responsibilities that have traditionally been theirs. It is particularly important that those who invite, welcome and teach the catechumens be grounded in the incarnational theology of Vatican II and its implications for a Shared Wisdom model of church. The Spirit calls the people, through us, to the church of tomorrow, not the church of yesterday. Incarnation continues!

Discovering the Presence of the Risen Lord

All conversion experiences are relational. We convert, change, grow, risk because someone has called, cared, loved, challenged, touched us. There are times when God seems to do that very directly, but most often it is through another person. This makes a great deal of sense as we recall that the Spirit is with us always and that each of us is given that Spirit for the good of all of us (1 Corinthians 12:8).

It is important here to return to that concept of the God of our lived experience. This is where the incarnate God, known through the wisdom of the Spirit, is to be found. Unfortunately, it is all too easy to miss this God on the daily journey. Too often we live our lives on automatic. How easy it is to wake up in the morning, push the "on" button and go through the day on "coast," only to come to the close of the day, gratefully find the "off" button and perhaps add a "Thank God I made it!" A valid prayer, no doubt, but not good enough for those of us called to be the presence of the risen Lord in family, church and society.

We need to pay attention to life, to process the action of the Spirit, to surrender to the presence of God in the daily events that we call life. We need to be in touch with our stories. We also need to share those stories and be graced by one another's stories. It is this kind of shared life that gently becomes shared faith. It is this kind of vulnerability that draws others to the word made flesh in the very real human condition of the contemporary world where we all live: this world and this church of promise and problem, of joy and tears, of hope and craziness!

Our Emmaus Journey

What does this say to teachers, preachers and sponsors? Two things. First: Call forth, listen to, treasure, respect and learn from the life and faith journey of the catechumen. This is a journey that has brought this person to a new question, a new depth, a new challenge. It is a precious history, a vital witness to the presence of the Spirit in human life.

Second: Share your own life of faith, your journey, and call other members of the parish to do the same. What is it like to be a member of this church? The catechumen will not find that answer in books or lectures. It is to be found in the stories of those who dare to call themselves the people of God. It is especially important that the catechumen be given ample opportunity to experience the hopes and the struggles of those involved in the many emerging lay ministries in today's church. In 1980 the National Conference of Catholic Bishops issued a document entitled, "Called and Gifted: The American Catholic Laity." At the conclusion of that document the bishops say:

> We are convinced that lay people are making an indispensable contri-
> bution to the experience of the people of God and that the full import

of their contribution is still in a beginning form in the post–Vatican II church.

It is today's catechumen who will join tomorrow's lay people to further shape the church and continue to incarnate the risen Lord. The call is not just to conversion as a one-time event but rather to the ongoing conversion of being and building church. This deeper meaning of life as a conversion process is critical to an understanding of what it means to embrace the church today.

It seems appropriate to conclude my reflections by recounting a familiar story from the Acts of the Apostles. Our first description of the philosophy of Shared Wisdom is found in a story about catechumens.

In Acts 15, the author describes the story of the First Council of Jerusalem. To understand the story, we need to consider Peter. Here is the man whom we identify as the first pope, the man chosen and prepared by Jesus—but a man, like all of us, with a vision limited by his own lived experience. Peter's initial understanding of Jesus led to his initial understanding of his own mission: that it was to the Jews. But Peter, like so many of us in the church today, is confronted by others whose vision and lived experience provide a broader concept of the church. Paul and those who minister with him recognize a call to the gentiles and have the experience of the Spirit working among them. Paul's conviction and Peter's confusion are understandable. Their wisdom in working through the dilemma is graced and serves as a model for all future conflicts in church.

What did they do? Peter convened the Jerusalem Council. And who came? "Paul and Barnabas and other members of the church. . . ." These latter must have been the converted gentiles who went to tell their stories. It was the wisdom that they shared that moved Peter and the other leaders of the church to a new vision and a healthier church.

May those of us who are involved with the catechumenate recognize the need to share wisdom, to hear the call of the Spirit and to be the presence of the risen Lord for one another as we carry on the mission of the word made flesh.

◆ *Mary Benet McKinney, OSB*

What Kind of
Spiritual Leaders
Does the
Catechumenate
Want?

HE RITE OF CHRISTIAN INITIATION of Adults (RCIA) provides a spiritual leader with excellent cues in directing and guiding inquirers, catechumens, the elect, neophytes or candidates for full communion as they strive to grow in prayer and spirituality. The texts of the RCIA contain a wealth of ideas, images, stories and models for that ministry.

For example, some of the riches of the Catholic Christian tradition of prayer are reflected brilliantly in the rite of the presentation of the "Our Father," a compendium of our theology. The nature of evil, the immense chasm between love and hate and the overpowering experience of being healed or being delivered from evil are all graphically depicted in the anointings, scrutinies and exorcisms. Clear and vivid biblical images in all the rites are vehicles that engage the heart. Focus on the sacred scriptures through the Sunday and weekday lectionary affords the richest resource for personal prayer and a spirituality that is genuinely biblical, ecclesial, trinitarian, liturgical and open to God's Spirit stirring in all of creation. The blessing of baptismal waters places the sacrament of initiation—and any spirituality that is true to it—in the context of a sacramental world: plant, animal, air, water, fire, every atomic particle revelatory of a God who loves and cares for all that has been made. Baptism, confirmation and eucharist, as their initiatory unity is upheld in the RCIA, lead to a life of prayer in the Spirit of Christ that makes us less vulnerable to the pitfalls of the past. The universal call to holiness is clear in the catechumenate. Membership in the church, the community of disciples at the table of the Lord, shines brightly throughout the process. The social nature of humanity — its solidarity and oneness — is clearly evident in the catechumenate as is the spirit of joy and the challenge to human maturity.

Beginnings

St. Paul's prayer for the community at Ephesus is a good way to begin our reflections on the importance of prayer and spirituality that permeates the catechumenate. He wrote:

> I kneel before God, from whom every family in heaven and on earth takes its name, and I pray that God will bestow upon you gifts in keeping with the riches of heavenly glory. May God strengthen you inwardly through the working of the Spirit. May Christ dwell through faith in your hearts, and may love be the root and the foundation of your lives. (Ephesians 3:14–17)

According to Paul, three graces underlie our life in God: God's self-giving through the Spirit, the indwelling of Christ in our hearts and the gift of love that leads us to be people of justice and peace. Paul's prayer disposes us time and again to receive these graces as we kneel in reverence and adoration before our glorious and merciful God.

How well the Ephesians understood Paul's teachings we do not know. But certainly these lessons are major and outline the essence of the Christian life. Lesser lessons were shared with me by a friend who sent me this excerpt from an editorial by Robert Fulghum in the *Kansas City Times*. I share them because they contain an implicit spirituality.

> Most of what I really need to know about how to live and what to do and how to be, I learned in kindergarten. Wisdom was not at the top

of the graduate school mountain but there in the sandbox at nursery school. These are the things I learned: Play fair. Share everything. Don't hit people. Put things back where you found them. Clean up your own mess. Don't take things that aren't yours. Say you're sorry when you hurt somebody. Wash your hands before you eat. Flush. Warm cookies and cold milk are good for you. Live a balanced life. Learn some and think some and draw and paint and sing and dance and play and work every day some. Take a nap every afternoon. When you go out into traffic, hold hands and stick together. Be aware of wonder. Remember the little seed in the plastic cup. The roots go down and the plant goes up and nobody really knows how or why. But we are all like that. Goldfish and hamsters and white mice, and even the little seed in the plastic cup. They all die, and so do we.

Would that our world lived these kindergarten lessons. Unfortunately, by the time most of us are in second grade we are caught up in cultural and social trends that break down human relationships and prevent growth in our spiritual lives. In the popular book, *Habits of the Heart,* the authors describe the radical individualism that penetrates every crevice of our society and, by osmosis, has worked its way into the faith community. A separation between one's public and private life now exists so that individuals fail to integrate their personal lives with the social duties and responsibilities. As we attempt to experience and share the catechumenate and to live the spirituality that it contains, we do so in a social milieu that is not hospitable to gospel values. This must be noted, lest we become naive or edge over into romanticism.

Given this context, the persistent call for us both individually and as a community is to ongoing conversion. Day in and day out we are called to put on the mind and heart of Jesus. Conversion takes place at the three foundational levels of our personal and communal lives: at the level of seeing, at the level of knowing and at the level of relating. Technically these are known as a metaphysics, an epistemology, an ethics. Through conversion we begin to take God's perspective and apply that vision to our culture. We judge all in the light of the master, Jesus the Lord. We are challenged to live justly, lovingly and compassionately.

There are always unredeemed areas in our minds and hearts, always unredeemed segments of our political, ecclesial and social systems that need to be purified. Jeremiah's image of the potter should be embedded in our hearts. Every day we are to go down to the potter's house and be shaped by the divine artist. Conversion is the heart of the matter in the catechumenate and in all of Christianity, because it calls us to the most basic elements of our faith journey: obedience and self-giving. Until we live those patterns, modeled by Mary and Jesus, we are still far from the kingdom of God.

In His Footsteps

Prayer and a spirituality that opens out to the whole world is manifest when God's concerns and God's priorities become our own. In Albert Nolan's *Jesus before Christianity,* there are three characteristics that reveal Nolan's understanding of the historical Jesus. These are solidarity, liberation and compassion. A brief analysis of each of these markings might help us to overcome the individualism of our day and to enter more deeply into the paschal mystery—the corridor of conversion—that makes us a new creation. Is this not one of the major goals of the catechumenate?

Solidarity. Jesus was one with the people and he desired that the people be one with him and the Father. Unity dominated the consciousness of Jesus, and this awareness lead to a specific lifestyle. No one was excluded from the Lord's concern and love. Solidarity is not just a cognitive notion, it is a felt reality. When one person suffered, Jesus suffered; when someone rejoiced, the Lord rejoiced. The "we-they" distinction was never in Christ's lexicon.

The desire for solidarity and oneness among people faces a harsh fact: alienation, brokenness, sin. As the banner reads: "Nobody has it all put together." We all come before the Lord seeking to be healed and longing for peace. Worst of all is the denial of our fragmentation. Something is terribly wrong, and we turn to God's reconciling power in Jesus to make us whole again.

Why did Jesus come? The Gospel of John says he came that "we may have life, life to the full" (10:10). He came that we might be one with the Father and one with each other. There is no authentic prayer nor genuine spirituality unless it concerns itself in a deep way with solidarity. Prejudice, bigotry, discrimination and racism are attitudes of mind and patterns of human behavior that directly oppose the gospel message.

Compassion. Underlying the longing for solidarity is the grace of compassion. Jesus is the compassionate one. He has entered into our experience from the inside and knows firsthand our joys and our sorrows, our laughter and our tears, our anxieties and our hopes. To be isolated, not to be in compassionate relationships with God and others, is to be near the precincts of hell. Compassion eradicates that mistake. We stand together so closely that other people's joys and burdens become our own. St. Paul is clear on this: "If you carry one another's burdens, then you fulfill the whole law of Christ" (Galatians 6:2).

Mother Teresa is a contemporary model of compassion. When awarded the Nobel peace prize, she was asked by a journalist whether or not she was ever overwhelmed by the numbers of people dying in the streets of Calcutta. She shook her head and said no! She was overwhelmed not by the numbers but "by one, by one, by one." Her compassion, based on truly seeing the plight of others and feeling their pain, leads to action. She and her community walk along that road to Jericho and relive the good Samaritan story. It's also the story of Jesus on the road to Calvary. It's a story of compassion.

Liberation. Prayer and spirituality are about freedom. Living in an addictive society we often are not even aware of the forces, inner and outer, that hold us in bondage. We think we are free when actually we are enslaved by the opinions of others, co-opted by the consumerism of our culture, guided by the mass media in both our consciousness and imagination. It is not unlike poor Charlie Brown who made a snowball and looked around for a target. Lucy passed by and warned Charlie that if he threw that snowball at her she would pound his head into the ground; if he decided prudently not to do so, she would spare his life. The last caption shows Charlie, snowball still in hand, saying that life is full of choices but he doesn't get any.

Each of us must seek the truth of his or her own freedom. Physically, many struggle with tobacco, food, drink; psychologically, many wrestle with fears, anxieties and discouragement. Even at the spiritual level, frequently we cling to certain graces or gifts rather than to the Giver of those blessings. In our more honest moments, we are not so free as we think. Jesus came with the liberating message of love and forgiveness, with the healing touch of mercy and gentleness, with the stirring gestures of total self-giving. Freedom is ultimately a gift that must be cherished and protected. A disciple's responsibility is a disciplined life for the sake of freedom. Christian freedom centers always on doing God's will, namely, love and forgiveness.

Jesus lived solidarity, compassion and liberation. As disciples we follow in his footsteps and come to know, with deep familiarity, the atmosphere of the Upper Room, Gethsemane and Calvary, those places where Jesus experienced and shared solidarity, compassion and liberation.

Intimacy

Each of us has favorite words: perhaps "orthopraxis," "circumference" or "gingerbread." A favorite spiritual word of mine is "connectedness." What does prayer do? It connects us to the Lord in a mutual dialogue and intimate sharing. It establishes and sustains a relationship, individual and corporate. Not to pray—that is, not to communicate with the Lord—means a diminishment or termination of a vital relationship. The quality of a relationship is dependent upon the quality of communication. Prayer is communication, a listening and responding.

But something there is that doesn't like too much connectedness. Fear of intimacy paradoxically reflects the great fear of being unbonded. While desiring union we also become anxious over the vulnerability that closeness requires. Therefore, prayer demands courage, the kind Zacchaeus demonstrated in climbing the sycamore tree. Without risk of intimacy we shall never grow in our spiritual lives.

Three things can pave the way for intimacy: silence, solitude, surrender. These three conditions of prayer are also the business of the catechumenate.

Silence. Carl Sandburg states that "To know silence perfectly is to know music." From another angle, to know silence perfectly is to know God. The silence of prayer is not merely the absence of external noise. Rather it is an internal silence that makes us receptive to a tiny, whispering sound. It is an inner stillness that allows us to hear our own heartbeat and the pulsation of creation. We must wrestle with our self-preoccupation and the multiple distractions of daily life. But with persistence and discipline, gradually we can come to that land of quiet where we discover the source of our giftedness as well as the redeemer of our flawedness. A dangerous land, this silent land of truth.

Solitude. Emerson claimed that Wordsworth had no master but nature and solitude. Solitude is a good master if it leads us to the Lord. There is a deep need within all of us for a modicum of geographical, psychological and spiritual solitude. We need all three types of "space" in order to understand our identity and our mission in life. Our culture draws us into the roar of the madding crowds only to find there a destructive loneliness. Christian solitude, coming apart so that we might bring wisdom and love back to the community, is necessary for quality communication. Prayer without solitude is a contradiction in terms.

Surrender. Pope John XXIII had as his episcopal motto: *"Pax et Obedientia."* Peace and Obedience. Or, in a paraphrase, the land of peace is gained by the road of obedience. Christian spirituality is about surrender; it is about abandonment to the will and providence of God. Is everything going "my way" (as the song from *Oklahoma* narrates), or are the words of the Lord's Prayer that "your will be done" our guiding force? In our more honest moments, many of us can claim very little obedience or surrender. Mary's *fiat* is alien to our ears and, worse, to our hearts. Much grace is needed to enter into prayer with a willingness to do whatever God tells us. A

Carmelite poet, Jessica Powers, writes about the essence of surrender in this way:

> Yes to one
> is often no to another
> here walks my grief
> and here has often been
> my peak of anguish
> yes is the one need
> of my whole life
> but time and time again
> law forces no
> spiked leaden ball
> up through my heart and lips
> rending as it arises
> leaving its blood and pain
> yes is the soft
> unfolding of petals
> delicate with surprises
> and billowing delight
> curve and caress
> out to the one or many
> I would guess
> heaven for me
> will be an infinite
> flowering of one species
> a measureless sheer
> beatitude of yes
>
> —Jessica Powers, OCD

Forms of Prayer

In our Catholic tradition, three basic forms of prayer are presented as available to everyone. The first is meditative prayer *(meditatio)*. Here the mind exercises a considerable amount of activity in attempting to break open the word of God *(lectio)* or analyzes an experience from God's perspective or seeks discursive understanding of some aspect of life. Often this form of prayer is nourishing and productive. But it is busy prayer in the sense that stillness and receptivity is quite minimal. As a basic guideline, whatever form of prayer is nourishing, stay with it.

Another prayer arises primarily from the heart. Sometimes called *oratio,* this form of communication with God is more affective than cognitive, more stirring than illuminative, more loving than knowing. The person at prayer here continues to exercise considerable control. Yet there is more mutuality and reciprocity than in meditative prayer. The will is more predominant than the mind.

A radical shift takes place with the third form of prayer known as contemplation *(contemplatio).* For St. John of the Cross this involves "loving attention." Here God's activity is supreme. Here the person at prayer is drawn into the mystery and held there without ideas or images, without control or self-preoccupation. Contemplation is not reserved to the mystics. Every baptized person is called to be contemplative, to be lovingly attentive to Reality, to be willing to be taken by a particular moment of beauty, truth, mercy or goodness to its very Source.

There is a danger in distinguishing forms of prayer. People might think that on separate days they will try one form or another when actually all three forms of prayer should be enjoyed in a single given period of prayer. For ten minutes a person discursively reflects on a passage from scripture or some life experience. Then, for several minutes the heart responds affectively to what is before one's eye and heart. Then, in the silence, the mind is quieted and the heart is stilled to allow God to enter more deeply and draw the soul into the divine presence. This basic rhythm allows us to make our prayer total and human. Sunday group sessions at which catechumens break open the word of God may follow this general rhythm effectively.

Obstacles to Prayer

As a catechumen, neophyte or veteran Christian, various obstacles will surface, blocking our goal of union with God. Holiness, the vocation of every baptized person, passes through the narrow gate. Spiritual obesity—losing the compass or spending too much energy on other values—blocks the passage. What are some specific obstacles that hinder our prayer life, making our ongoing conversion as a catechumen or baptized person less effective.

Atheism. John Courtney Murray, SJ, mentions three forms of atheism that infect our century. There is economic atheism by which we do our buying and selling without any reference to God. There is political atheism whereby decisions at every level of government fail to take into account a religious or moral perspective. Then there is academic atheism that blocks the deity from the classroom and from the minds and hearts of students. But do we dare mention a fourth atheism, religious in nature? Is it possible to do religion, as good, competent professionals but without an awareness of God's presence and power? Certainly a rhetorical question. Yet many of us might squirm as we read this passage from the *Pastoral Constitution on the Church in the Modern World:*

> Believers can have more than a little to do with the rise of atheism. To the extent that they are careless about their instruction in the faith, or present its teaching falsely, or even fail in their religious, moral or social life, they must be said to conceal rather than reveal the true nature of God and of religion. (*Pastoral Constitution,* 19)

Activism. This heresy is as tough as quack grass. Achievement and productivity are what provide identity for activists, not their innate dignity as sons and daughters of a gracious, loving God. Heavy scheduling in ministerial projects may dominate their apostolic life, leaving little or no time for relational matters, be that quiet moments of prayer or the nurturing of friendships. This is not to set up a false dichotomy between identity and function, relationships and ministry. Balance, of course, is in order, but on the pragmatic level it is easy in our time to sell our souls to the company record keeper. The roots determine the fruits. Our active life must be well grounded if the fruit we bear is to be lasting.

No Models. In any major segment of life, mentors and models are important. Our primary way of learning is by example. We must see a life lived if we are to believe in its possibility. The challenge is to be creative. If we cannot locate around us individuals of prayer, we may have to adopt some wisdom figure or saint of an earlier century to be our guide. Reading the lives of the saints and the biographies of people of prayer can stimulate our personal prayer powerfully.

Parochialism. Our prayer and spirituality must be broad and expansive. To limit ourselves narrowly to one level of spirituality is a pitfall we cannot afford. Three dimensions seek recognition and integration: First we are to have a personal relationship with Jesus our Lord. A question each of us must ask is, "Have I allowed the Lord to take up residency in my heart?" Indeed he stands at the door knocking, the response is up to us. (See Revelation 3:20.) Second, spirituality must be ecclesial. We travel as a pilgrim people and each individual life affects the whole. Ours is a community of faith. We live under the guidance of a single, loving God. But more must be said. Our spirituality has a cosmic, global dimension. Our faith must be one of justice, and therefore we are concerned about all peoples of all lands. Faith leads to mission. God calls us to reach out and to share the good news given to us and, in return, to accept from other religions and peoples the revelation that God has given to them. If we fail to reach out, we will be deprived as well as deprive others.

Our faith must be somehow connected with the political and economic, the social and cultural dimensions of our world. Otherwise our spirituality will be privatized and compartmentalized. The challenge is to keep one eye on humanity, with all its glory and shame, and the other eye on the Eternal. If that causes spiritual schizophrenia, so be it. Better to live with the ambiguity of reality than to embrace a false clarity that eliminates half of what is. We face obstacles to our spiritual growth with courage and trust in the Lord. Grace is stronger than death and in that love we place our hope.

Implications

1. Balance. In one hand we hold the *New York Times* and in the other, the Bible. We bring God's perspective to bear on our culture. Our challenge is to read the signs of the times in light of the gospel of

Christ. Always we must return to what God asks of us: "This is all that the Lord God asks of you and me, to act justly, to love tenderly, to walk humbly with our God." (Micah 6:8) Nothing more; nothing less.

2. Conversion. *Metanoia* must not be limited to personal conversion alone. Rather we must be keenly aware of those elements within our economic, political, social and ecclesial structures that cry out for reform. Hands-on ministry is beautiful and important, but there is also need for doing upstream ministry: a systemic ministry, one that goes to the source of oppression and exploitation and asks for God's healing grace.

3. Osmosis. Whether we like it or not, all of us are deeply affected by the culture in which we live. No one sits in a room filled with cigar smoke without being affected by it. No one lives in our cultures of cash, convenience and consumerism (see *Habits of the Heart*) without being influenced for good or ill. Our challenge is reverse osmosis. We must permeate every segment of our culture with gospel values and attitudes. The struggle will be fierce but worth every effort.

Conclusion

This hopeful realism is what a spiritual leader wants to offer to catechumens and to all members of the church. A trust in God's love through Jesus Christ in the Spirit—this is what inquirers, cathechumens, the elect, neophytes and the rest of us faithful desire and seek. The good news is the love God shows through Jesus Christ who rewards a hundredfold our trust and our surrender, now and in the reign of God to come. *Deo Gratias!*

♦ *Robert F. Morneau*

What Kind of Pastoral Team Does the Catechumenate Want?

MANY OF MY YEARS of involvement as a pastor in the adult catechumenate have been years of groping and growing. I have been searching for my role with the process of Christian initiation. At first this was a "one-man show," not much more than going public with my "convert making." I treated the Rite of Christian Initiation of Adults (RCIA) as a new label for old concepts and practices.

Remembering my practice of 1974 ought to embarrass me today, but it doesn't. You see, the rite itself provokes us into a new way of being the church and a new way of ministering as pastors. The catechumenate reforms us, makes us into the kind of pastoral leaders envisioned by Vatican II. If we pastors are open to document and ready to be converted ourselves, then the rite will lead us and our parishes into a renewed church and the call to minister within it.

How Do I Begin?

Pastors who want to start the catechumenate process often ask me how to begin. I always have the same answer: "Jump right in. Begin tomorrow. Don't wait for the perfect plan with clearly defined steps, roles and responsibilities. All of us, even those of us with years of experience, still are in search of better ways of making this document a living experience in our parishes."

I still am learning about the catechumenate, and most of my learning comes from being with and listening to inquirers, catechumens, the elect, neophytes and those catechumenal team members who see their ministry as something more than getting the job done.

Renewal and Leadership

The catechumenate points up for us a more pervasive problem with leadership in the church today. I am convinced that this process of initiation is not just one more aspect of church renewal; it is a paradigm for all renewal. The catechumenate is a way of being church and this way of being church ripples into every other aspect of our ministry as priests. This document models a Vatican II ecclesiology so clearly and so well that it radically alters our personal and corporate perceptions of ourselves as ministers and as the people of God. It gives vision and direction to our renewal efforts. It instills zeal and a sense of mission at a time when many priests are suffering from spiritual boredom. It calls for and demands a variety of ministers and shared responsibility at a time when many priests are suffering from burnout through overwork. It calls for sharing faith and making experience the locus of revelation at a time when many pastors are wondering what is next in a parish program for community building. The catechumenate is not a cure for all the sins of the clergy and ills of the parish, but it comes as close to that as any effort of parish life and renewal that I've experienced in the 25 years since ordination.

So let the catechumenate have its way with you. Open yourself to its power and enjoy the radical change in vision it provokes in you and your people. There is no way for a pastor to "play church" in the midst of a catechumenate. The process itself short-circuits sham, role playing and clericalism. Even more exciting for pastoral ministry today is the fact that the catechumenate begins to awaken some gifts that we pastors have left dormant for too long. In short, the catechumenate leads to the conversion not only of the unbaptized and the baptized-uncatechized: The catechumenate converts pastors. Conversion is at the heart of the catechumenate process. That is what it promises and, in my experience, it delivers.

A Vision of the Pastor

Before looking at the specific role of the priest in the catechumenate, it might be well for each of us to clarify our general vision for a renewed priesthood. This was a favorite pastime in the late 1960s and early 1970s. With emerging lay ministries, pastors began asking the question: "But what is my unique, irreducible and nontransferable role in the church?" Much has been written since, but most of us still admit that we are ministers in search of a clearer identity.

Even in the question of identity, the catechumenate models the church that is to be. In many ways the pastor plays the same role in a parish that the bishop plays in the diocese. The pastor is the minister of unity, the one who oversees the teaching mission of the church within the parish. The pastor nurtures, supports and unifies the various charisms of the faithful, either directly or through others. The pastor presides at liturgy. Some fear that this can lead to the pastor's ministry being merely cultic; this cannot be because for us liturgy is the celebration of all we are and all we are called to be as a people.

The primary task of the pastor is the coordinating of ministries. The pastor is an essential center in a ministering community. With others, the pastor calls forth, enables and supports ministers who come from the people. The parish has become the new seminary where ministers for today's and tomorrow's church are being formed. That formation involves human and spiritual growth and development, theological grounding in the tradition and the development of skills necessary to fulfill the ministry to which the people are called by God and the community. The pastor will not be able to do that alone. At every level of parish life, the pastor's goal will be to move these new ministers toward mutuality. The goal is neither dependency on the pastor nor total autonomy, but reciprocal relationships where all recognize each other's charisms.

The Pastor and the Catechumenate

That style of ministry is what the catechumenate envisions: mutual and interdependent (not "codependent," a term currently in use to describe unhealthy, clinging relationships) ministries. In the late 1960s I heard Sulpician Peter Circio speak of the pastor as a pinch hitter. That concept has served me well in parish ministry and in the catechumenate. Initially, the pastor may have to pinch-hit as catechist and spiritual director and perhaps even as director of the catechumenate. But a pastor must realize what pinch-hitting is. Pastors should be working themselves out of jobs, transferring ownership and responsibility through empowering others to fill those roles. This will not be misread as the pastor taking leave from the whole effort: A pastor must remain in the midst of the catechumenal team, with them in the deepest sense.

Urban Holmes, in *Ministry and Imagination,* suggests four images for the pastor that ring true to me. For the catechumenal team, the pastor is a *wagon master:* not a person who *has* authority, but someone who *is* authority, someone whose words and life elicit respect because they strike the chord of authenticity in the team members. Or the pastor may be *storyteller* in John Shea's sense of that image. This image is uniquely appropriate to a pastor's ministry with catechumens, for storytelling is what it's all about, and storytelling makes storytellers of storyhearers. Or the pastor is the *clown,* the fool for Christ's sake, a true believer who seems foolish by our world's standards. The image from Holmes that I relate to most is that of Jung's *mana-person.* The pastor must have confronted the chaos in some sense in order to be credible to the team and to the catechumens. He must have faced the demons and survived, returned like Ishmael "to tell the tale." Every catechumenal team needs such a mana-person in its center, a storytelling, foolish wagon master. That person is called pastor or shepherd or a host of other images. The pastor in the midst of a catechumenal team is pastor in the New Testament sense of that word. He is not a monk or cultist, not primarily a social critic, not one who has to dominate.

One year, after having empowered a variety of ministers for the catechumenate, I backed off, let go, turned it all over to the director and the team. Something went sour. I became "the presider at rites." But I did not know the catechumens. Liturgy must spring from our life together or it becomes magic and mere ceremony. The pastor must be with the team and with the catechumens, not to do a great deal, but to be with them, share with them. There is no reason why a pastor cannot continue to pinch-hit in spiritual direction, planning, catechesis and formation of team members or catechumens. This is not "making room" for the pastor, but recognizing gifts and utilizing them when necessary. In this regard great caution and care are needed in the beginning of the transfer of ownership and leadership. Many priests feel that they are better catechists or spiritual directors because of their experience. Letting go of these roles and giving other people the privilege of trying, and even failing, will develop their talents beyond those of a priest. This emptying is the kind of risk and dying that is necessary in the church that is coming of age.

Members of the Pastoral Team

After all these years of developing ministers for the catechumenate, I am able to see myself primarily as a necessary and essential member of the catechumenal team. I meet regularly with the director of the catechumenate and serve as a resource person to him. I help plan with the team, am a part of interviewing the catechumens and take part in their retreats. Most of the ministry now is in the hands of others, people of the parish who have developed their talents and minister in ways that I cannot. I see myself as a support and resource to the ministers, a planner with the team and one of the spiritual directors. This direct contact with the team and the catechumens enables me to celebrate the stages of the catechumenal journey with the people with whom I have shared my faith and whose faith has inspired me. It is a ministry of overseeing and coordination, a ministry that integrates the catechumenate into the entire life of the parish.

Most of all, the catechumenate has enriched my ministry as pastor and has given me a new perspective on all I do in the parish. Mixing with catechumens and ministers of the catechumenate leads to a conversion for a pastor. As the "Introduction" to the RCIA puts it:

> The initiation of catechumens is a gradual process that takes place within the community of the faithful. By joining the catechumens in reflecting on the value of the paschal mystery and by renewing their own conversion, the faithful [of which, this writer reminds the reader, the pastor is one] provide an example that will help the catechumens to obey the Holy Spirit more generously. (RCIA, 4)

That is the role of the pastor in the adult catechumenate, a converted exemplar who has not arrived yet, who still is on the journey and is ready to die again by letting go of old roles and old ways so that we as church might obey the promptings of the Holy Spirit in these days.

♦ *Thomas J. Caroluzza*

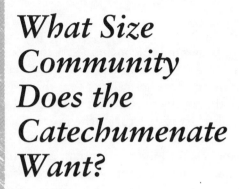

What Size Community Does the Catechumenate Want?

*I*F I WERE PRESSED to name *the* major problem with the way we practice the catechumenate in the United States, I would not hesitate to say it is this: Contrary to the text of the Rite of Christian Initiation of Adults (RCIA), initiating new members into the church is considered to be just one of many important activities of the parish, rather than a way of being the church for all members of the parish. In other words, the responsibility for the catechumenate has been turned over to the parish catechumenal team, instead of being the concern and business of all the baptized. (Cf. RCIA, 41)

Parish catechumenal teams are doing a good job. They have invested considerable energy and resources in moving the catechumenate from the convert class conducted by a few parish professionals to a model of evangelization and sharing faith led by a variety of ministers from the parish. But that excellent work has not been enough to transfer the ownership of the catechumenate to the people in the pews. Even in the best of parishes, most parishioners remain passive observers of the process of initiation.

Some who have had many years of experience with the catechumenate are beginning to conclude that the route to a fuller implementation is a structural change. They feel that the present structures of our parishes cannot bear the weight of that vision of the church that we were given in the 1972 and 1985 versions of the RCIA text. They are restructuring their parishes into a community of smaller communities. They see each one of those communities as having some responsibility for initiating new members.

There are other problems that have led some to explore a small-community structure for the catechumenate. One of these is our continuing insistence on being program centered, if not in method, then in timing. Another is the way that, in many parishes, the catechumenal team is becoming the real parish for the catechumens, a parish within the parish. People then are initiated into a committee, not into a parish. Our culture has a great fondness for surrogates. The catechumenate must resist using such substitutes to fulfill the responsibility that every Christian received at baptism.

The Small-Community Alternative

A small-community structure for the catechumenate, besides providing a solution to many of the concerns expressed previously, helps solve other problems: sponsorship, follow-up and the background diversity of inquirers and catechumens.

In the small-community model of the catechumenate, a resource team still is needed, but it does not exercise all the functions, roles and responsibilities in the process of initiation. The catechumenal team would *enable the small communities to fulfill this ministry.* Our Lady of Nazareth Parish in Roanoke, Virginia, and Our Lady of Lourdes Parish in Saskatoon, Saskatchewan, Canada, both have used the small-community model of the catechumenate for the past five years. Their model of parish need not be copied, however. No one has all the answers. I want to offer a few possibilities for parishes that see the small-community option as a way to implement the catechumenate more fully and more authentically and as a better way to give responsibility to all the people of the parish.

The assumption in what follows is that there are small communities in the parish or that the parish wishes to establish such communities. I see no need to wait until a parish has the complete plan in place. I would begin simply, but I would begin now.

A Vertical Approach

People in a small community have learned how to listen to each other and care for and support one another or they are not yet a community. Yet the members of the community know that they must get beyond self-nurture, reaching out at home, in their neighborhoods, at work and in recreation. They need to invite interested people to join them for prayer, in sharing experiences of faith, for ministry or in whatever it is that gathered them in the first place. Members of such communities then would help inquirers to raise questions. Members would be open to newcomers. In the language of the RCIA, the small group is the precatechumenate: the opening up of the spirit of the community to the inquirer. Here is the *first* proclamation of the living God, the *first* evangelization, the development of an *elementary* faith in Christ as one who fulfills the inquirer's spiritual expectations in the church.

When the small community discerns an inquirer's readiness to enter the catechumenate, the members would present the candidate to the parish catechumenal team and offer sponsorship. This would be done publicly at the rite of acceptance into the order of catechumens. In this model the small community need not participate in the second period, the catechumenate itself. In any case, one member of the small community would sponsor each catechumen and would have a much greater role in her or his faith development. That sponsor would share with all the members of the small community the catechumen's progress in faith. The members of the community would continue to offer support from afar in their continued friendship and informal contacts with the catechumens.

During Lent the candidate would return to the small community where prayer, fasting and works of charity are learned and practiced with the group. Members of the small community who have come to know the candidate will want to give testimony at the rite of election or enrollment of names and actively will be involved in the lenten rites and the Easter Vigil.

During Eastertime, the small community helps discern the gifts of the neophyte and how those gifts might be exercised in the parish and in the world. The tender faith continues to be nurtured in the small community in the months and years to come. There is little need for follow-up programs for new members in this model. The new Catholic is nurtured and supported by people whom he or she has come to know intimately over many months. When 20 or 50 smaller communities are exercising such responsibilities in this or a similar way, we can expect not only larger numbers of inquirers and catechumens each year, but greater numbers of parishioners directly involved in the process and the rites.

A Horizontal Approach

A different, but equally exciting, small-community model is for some parish communities to focus on precatechumenate and evangelization, while others focus on catechesis and still others on the content of the lenten and Eastertime activities. Within this model, a sponsor takes the inquirers and catechumens at different times for different reasons. After Eastertime the neophyte chooses one of those communities as her or his own, the people with whom she or he will minister and grow.

The advantage of this second model is with the greater number of parishioners whom the candidate comes to know over the many months of the journey. The disadvantage is that this experience is less intimate. Less bonding takes place between the candidates and the members. Those who support this second approach feel that bonding takes place better when the new Catholic chooses a stable community after Easter.

Small Communities as Supplementary

Some parishes have chosen the small-community model for supplementary and individualized catechesis. Both the Nazareth and

Lourdes parishes have taken this route. In this model the catecheti-cal needs of each catechumen are the primary concern. While group catechesis continues each Sunday after the dismissal, the special needs and interests of the catechumens are met by a small commu-nity that has come to have a special catechesis and formation focus. The sponsor may assume responsibility for bringing the catechumen to those communities for one or more sessions.

There are many more possibilities. These three are offered not as fully developed models but to stimulate the reader's own creative energy. Small communities draw emphasis from the team itself to the small community as the locus of energy. With that shift, a major problem of our initiation practice will be solved.

The catechumenate belongs to the whole parish, not just to a delegated surrogate. The small-community model of the catechu-menate may implement this vision of the catechumenate better than our present practice. It preserves the intimacy that we have found to be essential in the catechumenate while returning the responsibility of initiation to greater numbers of parishioners.

♦ *Thomas J. Caroluzza*

Afterword:
Seven Reasons Why Your Parish Needs a Catechumenate

HE RITE OF CHRISTIAN Initiation of Adults (RCIA) is not an option. Since the publication of the Latin typical edition for the universal Roman church in 1972 and the provisional translation in 1974 prepared by the International Commission on English in the Liturgy (ICEL), the RCIA has been the official rite to be used when preparing adult converts for the sacraments of Christian initiation: baptism, confirmation and first eucharist. At their November 1986 meeting, the U.S. bishops placed themselves squarely behind the RCIA by an overwhelming approval of the following agenda items: a final ("white book") ICEL translation of the RCIA, a series of adaptations to be used for the church in the United States, a list of national statutes and a national program for implementation of the catechumenate. The revision of the RCIA offers an improved translation and editorial rearrangement achieved primarily by shortening and combining the introductions to the various rites. More significant changes are found in the pastoral adaptations, which provide helpful distinctions to be made between the unbaptized (catechumens) and the already baptized (candidates) in the celebration of the rites. The converts or catechumens, properly speaking, are those for whom the RCIA is primarily intended. The candidates may be either uncatechized adult Catholics preparing for confirmation and eucharist or baptized Christians preparing to be received into full communion in the Roman Catholic church. By making this distinction between the unbaptized and the baptized the uniqueness of the sacramental character of baptism is respected and ecumenical sensitivity heightened. The 37 paragraphs of the national statutes clarify who the participants in the catechumenate may be and strengthen the catechumenal process, especially by suggesting a one-year catechumenate extending from Lent/Easter of one year to Easter of the following year. The national plan of implementation was an ambitious five-year blueprint of progressive realization within which the RCIA would be mandatory in every parish by the First Sunday of Lent, 1988.

The Holy See has approved these liturgical changes, thus opening the way to a full-scale implementation of the RCIA. On March 7, 1988, the National Conference of Catholic Bishops finally received the decree of the Congregation for Divine Worship confirming their approval of the ICEL white book translation and the ritual adaptations for the church in the United States. July 1, 1988, was the new publication release date; September 1, 1988, was the new mandatory effective date of implementation.

How will the revised RCIA be received by parishes? It might be useful to ask why a parish would want to have a catechumenate in the first place. Some parishes consider it an archaism that concerns only a handful of people and would prefer to revert to the earlier method of convert making. Many parishes really do not know what the RCIA is about, or they feel it is just one more program coming down the pike to be implemented by an already overburdened clergy. Other parishes have discovered what a blessing the RCIA can be for parish life and, as the bumper stickers enthusiastically exclaim, "I've found it!" a whole new vision of church unfolds before them. Here are seven good reasons why your parish would want to have a catechumenate.

A Catechumenate Strengthens
the Missionary Outreach of the Church.

In his book *Christianity Rediscovered* (Orbis, 1985), now into its fourth printing, Vincent Donovan recounts his efforts at evangelizing the Masai people in East Africa. Despite many years of a Catholic presence in schools and hospitals, converts were few. Donovan decided to leave the mission compound and to search out small groups of this nomadic tribe in order to tell them firsthand about Jesus Christ. He was startled at their initial response: "If this is why you came here, why did you wait so long to tell us about it?"

One does not have to journey to a distant land to ponder a similar question: What kind of impression are we, the church in the United States, making on contemporary society? With all the educational resources, social services and moral exhortations the church provides, does our culture perceive the very reason for what we do and who we are as Christians: the person of Jesus Christ, the new life in God the risen Lord opens up to us in the body of Christ and the love of Christ and the Holy Spirit that impels us?

In a post-Vatican II era that has experienced a veritable explosion of ministries, we so easily can neglect the basic Christian mission to evangelize. In his *The New Testament in the Life of the Church* (Ave Maria Press, 1980), Eugene LaVerdiere, SSS, writes: "Evangelization is the most fundamental of all ministries. Unless the gospel has been proclaimed and unless it has been heard and accepted, every other ministry is futile" (27).

Pope Paul VI saw the mission of evangelization in the widest possible perspective of bringing the good news to all strata of humanity and through its influence transforming humanity from within and making it new. The Paulist National Catholic Evangelization Association strives to continue this vision.

This missionary imperative and the catechumenate coincide especially during the first period of the RCIA: the precatechumenate or period of evangelization, a time for the first hearing of the gospel by inquirers. Archbishop Pilarczyk aptly describes the RCIA as the "liturgical expression of a fundamental responsibility of the local church to preach the gospel of Jesus Christ."

A Catechumenate Restores the Original Faith Process of Evangelization, Catechesis and Liturgical Celebration.

The origins of this process are found in those passages of the New Testament that describe the first instances of baptism in the primitive church. At the conclusion to Peter's Pentecost discourse in the Acts of the Apostles (Acts 2:37–42) and in virtually every succeeding chapter, a similar pattern obtains: evangelization leading to conversion, leading to baptism, leading to life in the eucharistic community of the church with a mission for the salvation of the world. Evangelization has to do with the fundamental credal statement that later found expression in the written gospels and creeds of the church: Jesus Christ is risen Lord.

Historically, the process of conversion later developed into the catechumenate, described by different writers as conversion therapy—how to survive a conversion—or the nurture of conversion in a context of hospitality. Various rites arose to mark the journey of faith of the catechumen, most notably these three: acceptance into the order of catechumens, election or enrollment of names and the celebration of the sacraments of initiation at the Easter Vigil. These steps or stages are not simply ceremonies to get out of the way or hoops through which catechumens jump. Rather, they are bridges or transitions that hinge together the successive periods of precatechumenate, catechumenate, lenten enlightenment and Easter mystagogy.

A few years ago catechists and liturgists were behaving like estranged partners whose marriage was on the rocks: liturgists reducing the ministry of catechesis to an exercise in classroom teaching; catechists writing off liturgy as a preoccupation with rubrics. The RCIA has reconciled catechists and liturgists who no longer work at cross-purposes, but now both see that the fundamental way the faith is handed on (*tradere*, tradition) is through telling the story of the good news of Jesus Christ and celebrating its meaning in the rites. This is why the catechetical instruction for the catechumenate is best drawn from the scriptural readings of the Sunday lectionary. This is also why the dismissal of the catechumens from the Sunday eucharistic assembly makes good sense: They are not being expelled from the community; rather, they are being sent forth with their catechists to ponder further the proclaimed scriptural word of the day.

A Catechumenate Focuses on the Liturgical Year and Revitalizes Lent, Easter and Pentecost in the Parish.

The church year is one of the most neglected features of the liturgical renewal. For many it seems to be a structure imposed on reality, a "liturgy land," having to do more with a static understanding of time than with people living the mystery of Christ. A recent circular letter from the Vatican Congregation for Divine Worship (January 16, 1988) sought to dispel this notion by drawing attention to the preparation and celebration of the Easter Vigil and Eastertime as the highlight of the liturgical year. To quote paragraph 7:

> The whole rite of Christian initiation has a markedly paschal character, since it is therein that the sacramental participation in the death and resurrection of Christ takes place for the first time. Therefore Lent should have its full character as a time of purification and enlightenment, especially through the scrutinies and by the presentations of the creed and the Lord's Prayer; naturally the Paschal Vigil should be regarded as the proper time to celebrate the sacraments of initiation.
>
> From its inception Lent has had to do with the initiation of new Christians and the recycling of the already baptized as all prepared for Easter. With the disappearance of the catechumenate in the sixth century, Lent remained a season of conversion but became more pronounced as a time for individual asceticism; the link with Easter and initiation was lost.
>
> Now Lent is being rediscovered as a season of communal conversion: a baptismal retreat with discernment and spiritual direction for

the elect in their final period of preparation for the Easter sacraments and a time for all members of the community to take seriously the challenge of Ash Wednesday by cooperating with the grace of God and by preparing to renew their baptismal promises at Easter. The Fifty Days of Easter constitute a season of mystagogy wherein the neophytes reflect on the meaning of their initiation as all members of the parish, new and old, seek to live out their baptismal vocation as a Pentecost community with a mission to the world.

A Catechumenate Replaces Private Instruction with a Progressive Integration into a Living Community of Faith.

In my first parish assignment in the days of one-on-one convert instruction modeled after *Father Smith Instructs Jackson,* I was often haunted by the prospect that the potential convert could conceivably be initiated into the faith without necessarily knowing any believers other than myself and the sponsor. The parish needs a catechumenate, but the catechumenate also needs a parish. The experience of the catechumenate, revived in France during the postwar years, has demonstrated this. The catechumenate was conducted at catechetical centers in Paris and Lyons. Unfortunately, the drop-out rate after initiation was staggering: The converts showed little staying power to persevere in their newfound commitment. We now know that the reason for this attrition was that the newly initiated had not been properly integrated into parish communities that could continue to nurture their faith. Once again Archbishop Pilarczyk wisely comments: "Becoming a member of the church is not so much a matter of knowledge as of participation in a community of believers."

A Catechumenate Stresses Formation as Well as Information.

The RCIA presents a model of catechesis that is holistic and multidimensional. In many parishes the catechumenate is modeled after the school year extending from September to May. We hope that the one-year catechumenate mandated by the national statutes will help dispel this academic model. The multidimensional catechesis is actually fourfold: doctrinal, communal, liturgical and apostolic.

Doctrinal formation means believing with the parish community. With proper preparation and discernment provided by resources such as *Breaking Open the Word* (Paulist, 1986, 1987, 1988), the Catholic doctrines that need to be handed on can be drawn from the scriptural selections of the Sunday lectionary.

Communal formation comprises the practical experience of living with the parish community in an incarnational way so that the catechumens come to perceive existentially what it means to be a Catholic Christian.

Liturgical formation, richly provided in the liturgies of the catechumenate, enables catechumens to pray with the parish community. This dimension is important because ritual prayer is likely to be an untouched and different experience for a newcomer.

Apostolic formation requires active service with the parish community. Perhaps the most vital component in any catechesis to adults or to children is the truth that we are Christians not only for ourselves but for others: We not only are saved; we are also sent.

A Catechumenate Offers a Model That Is Most Effective in Reaching Catechumens and All Members of the Parish.

After learning about the various backgrounds of people who may be included in a catechumenate, a student asked me recently when the church is going to provide a renewal process for those in full communion but uncatechized. Pope John Paul II seemed to have this need in mind when he wrote in *Catechesi Tradendae*, 44:

> Among the adults who need catechesis, our pastoral missionary concern is directed to those who were born and reared in areas not yet Christianized and to those who never have been able to study the Christian teaching that they have discovered at a certain moment in life. It is also directed to those who in childhood received a catechesis

suited to their age but who later drifted away from all religious knowledge because a rather childish kind of knowledge was all they had. It is likewise directed to those who feel the effects of a catechesis received early in life but badly handed on or badly assimilated. It is directed to those who, although they were born in a Christian country or in sociologically Christian surroundings, have never been educated in their faith and, as adults, are really catechumens.

Thomas Ivory, rector of the American College in Louvain, Belgium, has suggested a catechumenal process which could be adapted for parish renewal. While keeping both the terminology and membership distinct from the catechumenate, the process would correspond to the four periods of the RCIA. The period of evangelization would correspond to a time of outreach. The catechesis during the catechumenate would parallel Christian formation. The lenten enlightenment would become a time for spiritual reawakening leading to the renewal of baptismal promises at Easter. The Easter mystagogy would be a time for ministerial discernment and development.

A catechumenal model of preparing adolescents for the sacrament of confirmation is found in several preparation manuals, e.g., *"Be My Witnesses"* (William H. Sadlier, 1985), and in the guidelines of some dioceses, e.g., Paterson, New Jersey. The process of adaptation calls for great care to avoid terminology that equates baptized teenagers with unbaptized catechumens, to modify the terminology drawn from the RCIA and to recognize that confirmation is one of three sacraments of initiation together with baptism and first eucharist.

The catechumenal model has also inspired pastoral efforts aimed at reconciling estranged Catholics. In an intervention at the 1983 Synod on Reconciliation and Penance, Cardinal Joseph Bernardin advocated a modified order of penitents modeled after the RCIA. James Lopresti, SJ, has recently designed exactly such a process which he calls more felicitously "re-membering church" in his publication, *Penance: A Reform Proposal for the Rite* (Pastoral Press, 1987).

A Catechumenate Needs the Resources of the Parish and Becomes the Place to Develop All Ministries in the Local Church.

A parish community would be unable to sustain a catechumenate without first calling upon the resources of its parishioners. Of all the revised rites, the RCIA contains the fullest delineation of "offices and ministries." First mentioned is the all-important office of the parish community exercising a corporate sponsorship during the four periods and a corporate presence at the three liturgical steps or transitions. Then come the individual ministries: the sponsor/godparent who journeys with the catechumen; the bishop who coordinates the RCIA in his diocese and presides at the rite of election and later at a mystagogical eucharist for the newly initiated; the presbyters whose cooperation is essential if the catechumenate is to flourish; the deacons who assist; the catechist or director of the catechumenate, a ministry best entrusted to a layperson. Karen Hinman Powell, in *How to Form a Catechumenate Team* (Liturgy Training Publications, 1986), expands this list to the following ministries: hospitality, communication, liturgy planning, retreats, catechesis, prayer leaders, sponsor coordinator, spiritual companion or director, evangelization.

Pastors should not see the RCIA as one more responsibility they must take upon themselves. Rather, the catechumenate can be the impetus for a more collaborative style of pastoring that animates and facilitates the many gifts already existing in any parish community. Seasoned practitioners of the RCIA suggest reaching beyond the usual generous parishioners who seem to do everything and involving others not yet actively engaged in parish ministry.

Finally, the goal of the catechumenate is not Easter, but Pentecost. During the Eastertime mystagogy the neophytes have the opportunity to discern more clearly their gifts of service to the church and to locate a sense of mission and outreach in their lives. In this way they reenact once again what Ron Lewinski calls the ever-recurring process of being a local church. It is the lifelong and ever-deepening spiral of preaching the gospel that leads to conversion, that leads to baptism, that leads to eucharist, that leads to ministry and back again to preaching the gospel. These are the blessings the RCIA brings to parish life. This is why your parish wants and needs a catechumenate.

♦ *Charles W. Gusmer*

Authors

THOMAS J. CAROLUZZA, pastor of Holy Spirit Parish, Virginia Beach, Virginia, received his doctorate of ministry from St. Mary Seminary, Baltimore. He served on the national staff for Renew from 1984 through 1986 and offers a variety of workshops and seminars on parish ministries and liturgy. He has lectured on the catechumenate throughout the United States and in Scotland, England and Germany.

AUSTIN H. FLEMING serves as parochial vicar/campus minister at St. Ann University Parish and as Catholic chaplain for Emerson College in Boston. He received his master's degree in liturgical studies from the University of Notre Dame. His articles and reviews have appeared in *Pastoral Music,* NPM *Notebook, New Catholic World* and *Liturgy 80.* He has authored *Preparing for Liturgy: A Theology and Spirituality* and *Parish Weddings.*

CHARLES W. GUSMER, professor of sacramental theology and liturgy at Immaculate Conception Seminary, Seton Hall University, South Orange, New Jersey, authored *And You Visited Me: Sacramental Ministry to the Sick and the Dying,* for which he received world acclaim. His list of lectures, audiocassettes, articles and other titles on pastoral liturgy is of the highest quality, including his forthcoming book, *Worship: A Pastoral Approach.*

ROBERT W. HOVDA, priest of the diocese of Fargo, writes "The Amen Corner" as a regular feature of *Worship.* Among his many publications is *Strong, Loving and Wise,* a pastoral guide to presiding at liturgy.

RON LEWINSKI is director of the Office for Divine Worship of the archdiocese of Chicago. He is founder of the *Catechumenate: A Journal of Christian Initiation* (formerly *Chicago Catechumenate*), member of the catechumenate subcommittee of the Bishops' Committee on the Liturgy, and member of the steering committee of the North American Forum on the Catechumenate. Author of *Guide for Sponsors, Welcoming the New Catholic, How Does a Person Become a Catholic?* and many articles, he is a widely-sought speaker on the Christian initiation of adults and children.

MARY BENET MCKINNEY, OSB, is prioress of the Benedictine sisters of Chicago and a management consultant for church systems. She holds a doctorate in ministry. Her work has ranged from principal of schools and associate director of administrative services for the schools and parishes of the archdiocese of Chicago to professorial positions at the University of San Francisco and the University of Notre Dame. She is the author of *Sharing Wisdom: A Process for Group Decision Making.*

ROBERT F. MORNEAU is auxiliary bishop of the diocese of Green Bay, Wisconsin, Vicar General and minister to priests. He is author of *Discovering God's Presence* and eight other books on prayer and spirituality.

JAMES T. TELTHORST, priest of the archdiocese of St. Louis, is director of the archdiocesan Office of Worship.